THEOLOGY FOR PSYCHOLOGY AND COUNSELING

THEOLOGY FOR PSYCHOLOGY AND COUNSELING

An Invitation to Holistic Christian Practice

Kutter Callaway
and William B. Whitney

Ⓑ
BakerAcademic
a division of Baker Publishing Group
Grand Rapids, Michigan

Published by Baker Academic
a division of Baker Publishing Group
PO Box 6287, Grand Rapids, MI 49516-6287
www.bakeracademic.com

Printed in the United States of America

Library of Congress Cataloging-in-Publication Data
Names: Callaway, Kutter, 1979– author. | Whitney, William B., author.
Title: Theology for psychology and counseling : an invitation to holistic Christian practice / Kutter Callaway and William B. Whitney.
Description: Grand Rapids, Michigan : Baker Academic, a division of Baker Publishing Group, 2022. | Includes index.
Identifiers: LCCN 2021028091 | ISBN 9781540963024 (paperback) | ISBN 9781540965271 (casebound) | ISBN 9781493434701 (ebook) | ISBN 9781493434718 (pdf)
Subjects: LCSH: Pastoral theology. | Pastoral psychology. | Pastoral counseling.
Classification: LCC BV4012 .C28 2022 | DDC 253.5/2—dc23
LC record available at https://lccn.loc.gov/2021028091

Unless otherwise indicated, quotations are from the NET Bible® copyright ©1996, 2019 by Biblical Studies Press, L.L.C. http://netbible.com. All rights reserved.

Scripture quotations labeled KJV are from the King James Version of the Bible.

Scripture quotations labeled NIV are from THE HOLY BIBLE, NEW INTERNATIONAL VERSION®, NIV® Copyright © 1973, 1978, 1984, 2011 by Biblica, Inc.® Used by permission. All rights reserved worldwide.

Scripture quotations labeled NRSV are from the New Revised Standard Version of the Bible, copyright © 1989 National Council of the Churches of Christ in the United States of America. Used by permission. All rights reserved.

Scripture quotations labeled RSV are from the Revised Standard Version of the Bible, copyright 1946, 1952 [2nd edition, 1971] National Council of the Churches of Christ in the United States of America. Used by permission. All rights reserved worldwide.

Baker Publishing Group publications use paper produced from sustainable forestry practices and post-consumer waste whenever possible.

22 23 24 25 26 27 28   7 6 5 4 3 2 1

To the students, mentors, and colleagues
who continue to teach us and remain steadfast in loving
and walking beside us as we continue to learn

Contents

Introduction

Key takeaways from this introduction:

- You are already a theologian.
- Theology is a spiritually formative practice; it is something you do.
- All that you do takes place in the presence of God.
- All theology is contextual and develops over time.

As with so much of life, everything we really need to know can be found in Pixar films. In *Toy Story*, the now classic movie that started the entire franchise, Buzz Lightyear lands in the middle of Andy's room, much to the surprise (and chagrin) of all the other toys. Rex, the neurotic tyrannosaur, is one of the first to approach the otherworldly intruder with a question that might strike some as obvious but is quite telling given the circumstances: "What does a space ranger actually do?"[1]

Theologians are not nearly as cool as space rangers, but for many they are as mysterious and misunderstood as the laser-shooting,

1. *Toy Story*, directed by John Lasseter (Emeryville, CA: Pixar Animation Studios, 1995).

karate-chop-action Buzz Lightyear who suddenly appears in the middle of an already full toy bin. For many, it is not entirely clear what exactly it means to be a theologian, much less what the requirements are for someone who takes up the mantle of "theologian" as part of their personal or professional identity. In other words, when it comes to this thing called "theology," some form of the question that Rex asks Buzz always seems to be on the tip of everyone's tongue: What does a theologian actually do?

This book attempts to answer that question not so much for the inquisitive plastic dinosaurs in our midst but first and foremost for students of psychology. Its primary goal is to invite burgeoning psychologists (undergraduate students in particular but grad students and educators as well) to consider what it means to be a theologian and what it looks like to do theology as a psychologist. On the most basic level, it simply outlines some of the key terms and concepts necessary for engaging in theologically informed psychology. On another level, though, it explores how to move from Scripture and the Christian tradition to the practice of psychology (and vice versa) in ways that are both faithful and robust. In doing so, it dares to suggest that psychologists—whether students, researchers, educators, or clinicians—are always already doing theology. As a result, they are, in fact, already theologians.

However, what will become clear is that this endeavor called theology isn't simply about thinking or theorizing; it's something you do. As a tradition of inquiry (very much similar to the tradition of inquiry known as psychology), lived theology is not merely an academic discipline, nor is it a purely speculative enterprise. It is also not superficial biblical proof-texting. Rather, it's a fully embodied, embedded, and extended practice—a holistic, lifelong endeavor that emerges from the practitioner's cultural context, draws energy from their personal experience, and develops in conversation with the biblical text, the historic Christian tradition, and a local worshiping community. So the question isn't so much about whether you are doing theology as a psychologist or even when the most effective times might be to "integrate" it into your research program or clinical practice. Instead, the question is about the depth, rigor, and critical self-awareness you bring to a task in which you are always already engaged.

Why Theology Is Important for Vocation

Even for those who are fairly clear about what the theological task entails, it is still fair to ask why a psychologist would want to be theologically informed in the first place. Given everything else psychology students need to learn during the course of their studies, including both the mastery of certain domains of knowledge and the completion of countless hours of supervised clinical training, isn't all this talk about theology a bit superfluous—a nice but nonessential addition to an already full plate of more vital matters?

In an important sense, the remainder of this book represents our attempt to answer this core question in a way that is both rigorous and accessible. But what we can say at the present moment is that, if you are someone who identifies as a person of Christian faith, then everything you do—from school to work to recreation—takes place *coram Deo*, or "in the presence of God." In other words, theology matters for psychologists because, ultimately, it matters for everyone. From the standpoint of the historic Christian tradition, whether we acknowledge it or not, the whole of our lives, including each and every one of our individual life projects, is caught up in a deep and substantive relationship with God. It may not yet be clear whether psychology is your one true calling in life, but whatever it is you choose to dedicate your time, talents, and creative energies to, God is present and actively involved in the equation. And having an adequate theological vocabulary for articulating this reality is a key component in understanding your work as a psychologist (or any other endeavor, for that matter) not just as a job or a profession, but as a vocation.

The English word "vocation" comes from the Latin word *vocare*, which means "to call." Interestingly enough, *vocare* also means "to name," which is a helpful way to think about a Christian understanding of vocation, for it suggests that who we are meant to be—our central identity or calling—is intimately connected to how God has named us.

Once again, *Toy Story* offers a helpful picture of what this naming looks like. In this movie, we see this same idea at work in the way that Woody and the other toys are named. Their owner, Andy, has literally inscribed his name on their soles (the sole/soul pun is very much intended). In other words, their core identity and, by extension, their central calling is to be one of "Andy's toys." To live in line with this vocation, each toy seeks to bring joy to the one whose name is written on their sole.

It's not a perfect analogy (we are not toys, and God is not an eight-year-old kid), but it does shed light on the ways in which theology can give voice to that which might otherwise go unnoticed and unsaid. More specifically, for those of you called to be practitioners in any of the subdisciplines of psychology, theology provides both a vocabulary and a broader conceptual framework for coming to a deeper understanding of the name that marks your identity as a beloved child of God.

That being said, a theologically informed approach to psychological research and clinical practice is about more than simply coming to an understanding of psychology as a legitimate vocation for Christians to pursue. It's also about the various "theo-logics" that orient and guide the discipline of psychology, even for those who are not Christian psychologists. Whether it's psychology's understanding of what it means to be human (i.e., anthropology), its notions about the coherence and predictability of the natural order (i.e., creation), or its take on how (and whether) the human spirit is related to other human and nonhuman spirits and, perhaps, even to the Spirit of Life (i.e., pneumatology), numerous theological assumptions are in operation at every level of psychological theory-building, research, and intervention. Thus, by developing a greater awareness of and competency with the theological tradition, psychologists are able to equip themselves not only with a deeper understanding of how certain theological assumptions inform the practice of psychology but also with a capacity to make these assumptions transparent and publicly available so that they can be critically scrutinized by the broader psychological community.

As with any human endeavor, scientific or otherwise, the problem is not that psychology operates according to a set of methodological assumptions or theoretical commitments. Those cannot be avoided. The problem is when these operative assumptions go unacknowledged and uncritically embraced—that is, when they become unassailable dogma.

A related problem has to do with how and, on a deeper level, what it even means to "integrate" the seemingly conflicting methodologies and theoretical frameworks of theology and psychology. A growing number of educators, scholars, and practitioners have proposed unique, often competing visions for the integration of these two disciplines. Nearly every one of these contributions has come almost exclusively from psychologists who are sincere and faithful Christians but who are not trained (or practicing) theologians. As a result, much of the psychology/theology integration literature is not only *not* integrated (because theologians are often not involved) but also suffers from somewhat thin and underdeveloped notions of the available theological resources and of the possible contributions that theology might make to psychology.[2] Another consequence is that psychology faculty who are teaching integration courses in the context of Christian higher education are increasingly voicing a common set of foundational questions: (1) What exactly are we doing when we do "integration"? (2) How do we do it? (3) Where do we start? and (4) Where are the resources?

Our hope is to address these concerns (along with a host of others that will arise as each chapter unfolds) by offering a more compelling case not only for *why* students of psychology would do well to develop their theological skills but also for *how* they might go about doing so. Of course, we won't be able to provide an exhaustive account of how one might engage in a more theologically informed

2. The end result, as Steven J. Sandage and Jeannine K. Brown helpfully point out (and attempt to correct), is an odd sort of insularity and self-referentiality within the integration literature. For instance, "two of the views in the *Psychology & Christianity: Five Views* (Johnson, 2010) book are represented by co-authors (a philosopher and psychologist in both cases), however it is noteworthy that none of the eight contributors to this key volume is a biblical scholar or theologian in terms of formal academic training." *Relational Integration of Psychology and Christian Theology: Theory, Research, and Practice* (New York: Routledge, 2018), 10. What is more, as Brad Strawn and his colleagues have noted, the Reformed tradition has been overrepresented among the practicing psychologists contributing to the integration literature, which has led to a "generic Reformed perspective" that has further narrowed the range of theological paradigms entertained by integrationists. Brad D. Strawn, Ronald W. Wright, and Paul Jones, "Tradition-Based Integration: Illuminating the Stories and Practices That Shape Our Integrative Imagination," *Journal of Psychology and Christianity* 33, no. 4 (2014): 300–310.

approach to psychology (or a more psychologically informed approach to theology, for that matter), but we do have in mind four interrelated goals that will, at the very least, get us moving in the right direction. More specifically, in this book we aim to do the following:

1. Introduce undergraduate psychology students to some basic theological terminology and concepts
2. Lay out a "method" for theological reflection that informs the practice of psychology in both clinical and research settings
3. Identify, develop, and deepen the key theological doctrines that operate in the background of the practice of psychology and are essential for engaging in theologically informed psychology
4. Upgrade the biblical and theological content of so-called integration efforts, focusing in particular on the ways in which theology deepens psychologists' understanding of their particular field and their work, whether in their clinical practice, in their research projects, or in their explicitly integrative endeavors

The structure of the book follows quite naturally from these basic goals. Part 1 considers what it means to do theology and why it matters for students of psychology. We begin with a discussion of theological method (chap. 1), and from that starting point move into an exploration of God's trinitarian relations with the created world (chap. 2), the presence and activity of God's Spirit outside of the church (chap. 3), and finally human beings as made in the image of God (chap. 4). Part 2 shifts from theology "proper" to a more direct exploration of the practice of psychology. Building on the theological framework established in the preceding section, in part 2 we focus on the various metaphysical assumptions that undergird psychological research, first by reimagining the task of psychology as a creative capacity to shape creation and to steward and name aspects of creation (chap. 5). The following chapter considers the practice of clinical psychology as a collaboration with the Spirit of God, and the person of the psychologist as a contextual theologian (chap. 6). The final chapter (chap. 7) proposes that one's vocation as a Christian within the work of psychology is part of a larger calling to find and develop areas of truth regarding the human person and human behavior that might lead us toward wholeness.

Theology as Spiritual Formation

In order to talk in any meaningful way about what theology is, we first have to unpack the preconceived ideas and misconceptions about theology that all of us bring to the table. Depending on your context, "theology" may be a somewhat neutral (or even meaningless) term. For others, it may function more like a four-letter word used to describe an unhelpful and out-of-touch group of old guys with gray beards obsessed with answering questions no one is asking. So to get at what it means to do theology, we first have to say a bit about what theology is not. The following "theology is not" list is by no means comprehensive, but it does name a few of the most prominent misconceptions we encounter when talking about theology in our classrooms.

- Theology is not simply a reinforcement of what Christians already think and/or believe.
- Theology is not merely or only an elaboration of what the Bible says—as if we could simply pluck out bits of data from the Bible and "apply" them directly to our context.
- Theology is not a purely intellectual task or academic discipline that takes place in an ivory tower filled with professionals called "theologians."
- Theology is not an "orthodoxy test" (or a heresy detector) that requires you to check a few predetermined doctrinal boxes so that you can go about your business as usual.
- Theology is not google searching for biblical passages that conveniently align with or reinforce ready-made psychological constructs.

Now that we've gotten that out of the way, let's move in a more positive direction and consider for a moment what theology is, or at least how we will be using the term throughout the book. First and foremost, theology is a lived wisdom. It's something you do, and not merely a way to think about or cognitively process information about God. It's a fully embodied, embedded, and extended practice in which one roots oneself in a living, historic tradition—specifically the wisdom traditions of the Judeo-Christian faith. To do theology is thus to join a dynamic and ever-emerging conversation thousands of years in the making about who God is, who humans are, and what God is up to in the constantly in-flux world we inhabit. As such, theology is a lifelong journey. No theologian ever "arrives," just as no theological claim is ever final. Everything is provisional because we're always engaged in a process of spiritual formation that develops over time, which may sound a bit counterintuitive at first, but it's really what makes theology both exciting and evergreen.

The English word "theology" comes from the Greek *theo* (god) and *logos* (word), so it literally means words or speech about God. But theology is not merely an attempt to describe God with language or to find the right propositional terms to define God in increasingly precise ways (although it often includes these things). Neither is it a matter of simply increasing our knowledge about God. Rather, theology is about knowing God. As Martin Buber would say, it involves an "I-Thou" encounter.[3] It's a relational endeavor in which we commune with the One who is present wherever "two or three are gathered in my name" (Matt. 18:20). To be sure, we certainly need and want to talk about this encounter in faithful ways—to put words to our experience so that we can understand it more fully and communicate it to others more effectively. But in many cases, the words that are best suited for doing theology are neither descriptive nor prosaic. They are poetic. They come in the form of prayers, songs, stories, rituals, and numerous other utterances. This kind of theology can also take the form of pictures, paintings, and musical pieces that are "too deep for words" (Rom. 8:26 NRSV).

To come at it from a slightly different angle, doing theology is also about orthodoxy, but only in a qualified sense. For many, orthodoxy is about maintaining the status quo. From this perspective, to be orthodox is to align one's beliefs with a clearly defined set of

---

3. Martin Buber, *Ich und Du* [I and Thou] (Leipzig: Insel Verlag, 1923).

positions deemed appropriate or acceptable by an institutional authority (religious or otherwise). If your beliefs line up and you believe them "rightly," you're in. If not, you're out (and you're a heretic!).

But theological orthodoxy is about so much more than that. Like the word "theology," the word "orthodoxy" comes from the Greek *ortho*, meaning straight, and *doxa*, meaning glory. So being and becoming theologically orthodox is not simply about aligning one's beliefs with a series of doctrines thought to be correct or true. Just as one goes to the *ortho*dontist to straighten one's teeth or sees an *ortho*pedic surgeon to straighten one's bones, joints, and ligaments, theology is about getting one's "glory" straight. To do so, we certainly have to increase our knowledge about God, but theological data alone will never be enough. To straighten our glory, we cannot pretend as if we are hard drives with skin in need of the latest operating system update, for theological orthodoxy involves nothing less than aligning and directing the whole of ourselves toward God— our thoughts, feelings, emotions, perceptions, attitudes, behaviors, practices, and, yes, even our propositional beliefs.

This notion of theology as a spiritually formative practice that involves getting our glory straight is key to understanding not only what theology is but also how you might go about doing theology in your context and in light of your calling as psychological scientists and therapists. Indeed, if you take away nothing else from this book, our sincere hope is that you are able to recognize that *everything* you do—whether as a clinical psychologist or a case worker or a spouse or a child or an artist—is always already theological. Again, it's not about whether you're doing theology but rather the degree to which you are doing theology in a life-giving, critically reflective mode. Both your person and your work training as psychologists strike at the heart of this larger project we call "theology." Indeed, they are integral to it.

Theology as Embedded (in a Cultural Context)

It is probably fair to assume that readers of this book will have had various and wide-ranging experiences with theology, anywhere from none at all to a lifetime of exposure. To account for this diversity, one of our strategies will be to try our best to make the familiar strange and the strange familiar, which may be a bit unsettling for those of you who explicitly identify as part of the Christian tradition. The reason for this is because by naming and in some cases challenging the theological assumptions that shape the way we think about psychology as a discipline and our work as psychologists, what we are really doing is making visible the many ways in which the particular sociocultural-historical contexts in which we are embedded (over)determine much of our theology. In other words, rather than proceed as if our understanding of God, our fellow humans, and the world in which we live reflects a universal and timeless truth, we are intentionally bringing to our collective attention the irreducibly contextual nature of all theology, and this can be particularly threatening for those who benefit from the totalizing visions of certain theological programs.

To set your mind at ease about what all this means, allow us to offer a few clarifying points. We are not suggesting that God is limited or time-bound but rather that our *perception* and *knowledge* of God are. As the apostle Paul says, "For now we see through a glass, darkly; but then face to face: now I know in part; but then shall I know even as also I am known" (1 Cor. 13:12 KJV). This is not necessarily a bad thing; rather, it is simply the case that, as humans, our basic awareness of the world is constituted by the particular histories we have inherited and the unique contexts in which we are embedded. In fact, this diverse and radically particular mode of being—the very thing that makes us human—is not only beautiful but also a living sign of the kingdom that is to come (Rev. 7:9–12).

The problem is not that we each embody a diverse set of intersecting cultural identities (e.g., ethnic, linguistic, racial, gendered), practices (religious, aesthetic, political), products (artifacts, tools, works of art), and structures (socioeconomic, ideological, technological). Embodying this set of cultural identities is just what it means to be human. The trouble comes when we become blind to (or altogether deny) the fact that our cultural context both enables and limits our theological vision or, worse yet, when we allow a culturally idiosyncratic view (usually our own) to function as the standard by which all other theologies are judged. When this takes place, "my" theology suddenly becomes capital-T "Theology" and everything else becomes some sort of derivative—a lesser version of the real thing.

Thus, as both Christians and psychologists, we must be vigilant in asking the question of how our own cultural context informs and constrains our theological and psychological projects. In some cases, it will be theological resources that are best suited to help us identify, describe, and unpack some of these culturally conditioned perspectives. In other cases, it will be psychological tools that will help us the most. Either way, it is crucial that we not only maintain an awareness of the contextual nature of all theology but also adopt a fiercely self-critical posture toward our theologizing. We also need to take the next step and educate ourselves about cultures that are "other" than our own, especially if we are part of a dominant culture prone to totalizing claims. Perhaps even more important, though, as we each develop our cultural competency, we must do so with a deep and abiding sense of what psychologists call "cultural humility"—the recognition that we all have gaps in our knowledge about what it's like to experience the world as a person from a culture other than our own.[4] Indeed, this describes the fundamental posture we want to assume in this book.

As two White, cisgender, heterosexual males, we want to acknowledge the profound ways in which our social location informs our understanding of theology and psychology (not to mention reality as a whole) and also call attention to the fact that we are indeed limited by gaps in our knowledge. We are continually attempting to increase both our multicultural competency and our cultural humility, which, much like theology, is a lifelong endeavor that has no end point. But in the spirit of the kind of cultural humility we hope to model in this book, our intention is to adopt a stance of not knowing, accepting that our ability to understand the culture and experiences of others is limited. Acknowledging our limitations means that, while we have no other choice but to speak from the particular locations we inhabit,

4. Dean M. Abbott, Noelany Pelc, and Caitlin Mercier, "Cultural Humility and the Teaching of Psychology," *Scholarship of Teaching and Learning in Psychology* 5, no. 2 (2019): 169–81.

we can do so in as self-aware and as self-critical a way as possible. At the same time, recognizing that ours is neither the normative nor default position means that we must at every turn draw on voices that originate from a location other than our own—decentering from the very start this shared project we call theology. To do otherwise would be to engage in a willful act of self-blindness. Indeed, it's one thing to accept that none of us will ever see perfectly, and then to move forward knowing we need others to correct our vision. It would be quite another to close our eyes ever more firmly without regard for how our groping about in the darkness is wreaking havoc on the lives of everyone around us.

As it concerns our own development as scholars, each day brings with it a renewed and ever-deepening sense of our many blind spots, which is why we will forever be indebted to the various women and people of color whose research, teaching, and scholarship have indelibly shaped not just the content of this book but our very lives as well. It is also why we have worked with a diverse team of scholars to develop a series of supplemental resources that will not only fill in the knowledge gaps that pervade this book but also generate critical insights that would otherwise remain inaccessible to us. We both hold PhDs in theology and terminal degrees in psychology (Kutter has a PhD in psychological science; William has a degree in marriage and family therapy and is in the process of completing a PhD program in psychology), but these qualifications do not in any way mean that we are somehow immune to the same kind of blindness that we all bring to the task of doing theology. In some important respects, these qualifications make us more and not less susceptible to mistaking multicultural competency with cultural humility.

Nevertheless, given our ongoing interest in developing a more robust collaboration between psychology and theology, we both feel called and compelled to help you deepen and upgrade the theological content with which you operate as psychologists. But the journey will produce fruit only if we keep our eyes wide open to the reality that our theology, like all theology, is deeply contextual and, in doing so, remain doggedly committed to listening to and learning from those who have the eyes to see what we cannot.

Theology as Developmental and Traditioned

It will be important to keep the inescapably contextual nature of theology in mind not only as we explore in greater depth what it means to do theology but also as we consider what it means to engage in clinical work in a pluralistic world where both psychologists/therapists and clients bring infinitely complex webs of overlapping and intersecting cultural identities to the table. In certain important respects, this kind of complexity is exactly what we should expect to encounter as theologically informed psychologists, for a genuine lived theology is ultimately about the whole of our life in the world, which is both richly diverse and unimaginably complex. Of course, simply knowing that life is complicated doesn't make our task any easier, but if we have any hope of effectively navigating the many spaces where the theological rubber meets the road, then it is vital that we come to a realistic assessment of the facts on the ground.

So rather than ignore or otherwise avoid these complexities, we are going to encourage you to lean into them and see them as an opportunity for growth and development. Indeed, one of the main reasons we are moving toward a more constructive approach in this book is because the task of doing theology is something that develops over time. We are constantly working out our beliefs/faith as we move through life with all of its various experiences. For instance, you probably thought about psychology and your faith very differently before you began your undergraduate studies in psychology. And five years from now you will think about psychology and your faith differently (hopefully in more complex, thoughtful, and humble ways). How our theology intersects with psychology is not always static because our views of self and God, much like our understanding of psychology, are not static. Ideas about God, psychology, science, and ourselves continue to develop as we live life and learn more. This speaks to how practicing theology is *developmental* in nature. As we make a concerted effort to grow in our Christian faith *and* expand our knowledge of psychology, we think about both our faith and psychology differently.

Like any other skill, learning how to do this well (i.e., in a contextually informed and culturally humble way) takes practice, which means that it's not enough to simply read books about theology, to memorize a bunch of technical terminology, or even to watch an expert perform at the top of their game (although all these are great things to do). Somehow and in some way, we must translate our knowledge into embodied action (and continue to do this over time); otherwise, our theology will remain forever abstract and inert, untethered from any real-world consequences.

There are of course numerous theologians out there who couldn't care less whether their theological projects speak to the concrete concerns of actual people. But that's not us. Nor is it reflective of our approach. More importantly, as students of psychology—a discipline that has as its central focus the thoughts, feelings, and behaviors of flesh-and-blood human beings—we don't think it should be your approach either. And that's because, to reiterate, theology is a lived practice before it is anything else. Knowing certain pieces of information is both important and necessary, but to quote a philosopher from the sixth century BCE, "One must learn by doing the thing; though you think you know it, you have no certainty until you try."[5]

An example taken from experimental psychology might help to make our point. In a recent study, a team of psychologists asked one group of participants to watch videos on YouTube featuring experts doing things like dart throwing, moonwalking, or playing video games.[6] The researchers had another group watch no videos at all. Afterward, all the participants were asked to perform the same set of activities. Just as expected, even though one group of participants knew every detail of every step because they had watched the YouTube videos, they were no better at actually doing these tasks than the individuals who hadn't watched the videos. In and of itself, that's not an incredibly interesting finding. What is interesting is that the people who had acquired knowledge about how to perform these activities by watching YouTube experts (but without the benefit of practice) consistently believed and perceived that they would, in

5. Sophocles, "Trachiniae," in *The Dramas of Sophocles Rendered in English Verse, Dramatic and Lyric,* trans. George Young (London: Sagwan Press, 2015), 191.

6. Michael Kardas and Ed O'Brien, "Easier Seen Than Done: Merely Watching Others Perform Can Foster an Illusion of Skill Acquisition," *Psychological Science* 29, no. 4 (2018): 521–36.

fact, be able to perform the skill well. To put it in the words of the psychologists who conducted the study, "People's actual abilities—from throwing darts and doing the moonwalk to playing an online game—do not improve after merely watching others, despite predictions to the contrary."[7]

It is precisely for this reason that, while training to be a psychologist/therapist, it's not enough to simply read books about therapy or acquire as much information as possible about different models of psychotherapy (although, again, these are important components to one's development as a psychologist). Instead, at some point, you have to *do* therapy. There simply is no replacement for putting our knowledge about the psychological dynamics of the human person into practice.

For instance, no one would say that because a person enrolled in an introductory psychology class in college, or grew up the child of a psychologist, or even read the *Monitor on Psychology* religiously, that they are somehow capable and equipped to go out and practice clinical psychology on an unsuspecting public. While these life experiences are important and need to be acknowledged as invaluable resources that can inform one's education, the only way to be and become a practitioner of clinical psychology who is capable of providing mental health services that are both responsible and life-giving is to listen to and learn from the hard-won wisdom of those who have gone before you—to sit at the feet of veteran clinical psychologists so that one day, in the not too distant future, you will be able to engage in the practice of psychology with equal parts confidence and humility.

The good news is that you don't do any of this alone or in a vacuum. Instead, your initial forays into therapy all take place under the watchful supervision of a practiced (and practicing) clinical psychologist. In fact, even after finishing all the required coursework for a doctoral degree, the state mandates that psychologists pass multiple postdoctoral exams and complete thousands of hours of supervised clinical training before receiving their license. But that's not the end of it. Even with a PhD and license in hand, clinical psychologists are required to complete a certain number of continuing

7. Kardas and O'Brien, "Easier Seen Than Done," 521.

education credits each year in order to maintain and renew their license.

Our point in outlining all these requirements is not to overwhelm you with a laundry list of obligations, or in any way to discourage you from pursuing your calling as a clinician. Fulfilling these requirements is well worth the time and effort. Our point is rather that to walk through the developmental process of being and becoming a practicing clinical psychologist is to commit oneself to being and becoming traditioned. Much like their theological counterparts, psychologists are participants in what Alasdair MacIntyre would call a "tradition of enquiry."[8] As a discipline, psychology has a commonly agreed on set of shared practices aimed toward a particular telos, or goal. So to become a psychologist isn't just about finding a job that's the right fit, nor is it simply about acquiring a set of technical skills; it is a dynamic, ever-emerging, lifelong pursuit—a traditioned way of being in the world.

Interestingly enough, the very same thing is true about theology, which is why we are approaching it as a similar kind of traditioned practice. In spite of the way academic theologians are trained in the late-modern West, there are clear parallels here to psychologists whose work as mental health professionals is known as their clinical practice. Few readers will likely take issue with this way of framing clinical psychology—as a living tradition constituted by a constellation of practices that a broad community of practitioners agree must be learned and embodied by anyone who wants to participate in the tradition. But if we said the same about theology, some might balk (or at least look at us with a raised eyebrow). For instance, you may go to church every week and faithfully lead your Bible study. You may be the child of a pastor or missionary or church planter. You may have even gone to a Bible college or seminary and received a degree in theology or biblical studies. But none of that on its own constitutes what it means to practice theology—to be and become a competent practitioner of theology.[9]

---

8. Alasdair MacIntyre, *Whose Justice? Which Rationality?* (Notre Dame, IN: University of Notre Dame Press, 1988), 79–80.

9. We are both from a tradition that affirms the priesthood of all believers and that all Christians (perhaps even all humans) are, in fact, theologians. However, we are drawing a distinction here between formal and folk levels of both psychology and

These are theological activities to be sure, but just as we wouldn't confuse the activity of reading a psychology textbook with the actual practice of clinical psychology, neither should we mistake reading a book about theology with the actual doing of theology. Which brings us back to the question with which we began: What does a theologian actually do?

The most direct answer is that theologians commit themselves to a lifetime of engaging in a formative set of practices that constitute the historic Christian tradition. But the more impressionistic answer is that they sit at the feet of a "great cloud of witnesses" (Heb. 12:1) in order to do theology in a way that is deeply rooted in and informed by the tradition they have inherited. Either way, they are joining a centuries-old conversation, listening to and learning from the hard-won wisdom of those who have gone before them.

This book serves as an open invitation for you to join that conversation—not as a side project that somehow needs to be incorporated into your psychological endeavors, but as something that stands at the core of what you do and who you are as a student of psychology. Of course, because we are theologians and not space rangers, we can't promise that our approach will take us "to infinity and beyond," but we do think it's a pretty good place to start.

Questions for Reflection and Discussion

1. Prior to reading this introduction, how would you have defined "theology"?

2. How would you describe the ways in which theology matters for psychology (if at all)?

3. Is there a specific theological tradition that you have inherited? If so (or if not), how do you think that informs your understanding of the theological task?

---

theology. Just as Sandage and Brown note, "Theology and psychology are formal scholarly disciplines, but at a more basic folk level everyone is both a theologian and psychologist . . . since everyone holds assumptions, however implicit, about ultimate concerns (theology), and everyone also engages in observations about people and the world around them (psychology)." *Relational Integration*, 11.

4. Does the idea that you are already a theologian strike you as odd, daunting, or exciting? Why or why not?

Resources for Reading and Exploration

Reyes, Patrick. *Nobody Cries When We Die: God, Community, and Surviving to Adulthood*. St. Louis: Chalice Press, 2018.

Sandage, Steven J., and Jeannine K. Brown. *Relational Integration of Psychology and Christian Theology: Theory, Research, and Practice*. New York: Routledge, 2018.

Yong, Amos. *Learning Theology: Tracking the Spirit of Christian Faith*. Louisville: Westminster John Knox, 2018.

PART 1

What It Means to "Do" Theology and Why It Matters for Psychologists

How to Do Constructive Theology

Key takeaways from this chapter:

Key takeaways from this chapter:

- Theology is something you do; it involves seeing the world with wisdom and discernment.
- The theological task involves at least five resources (Bible, church, tradition, experience, culture).
- Doing theology is a dynamic process and not a set procedure.
- Along with numerous other cultural forms, psychology serves as a critical resource for doing theology.

As a kid, I (Kutter) had terrible eyesight. I just didn't always know it. In fact, I distinctly remember the moment I realized how bad my vision really was. My parents were driving me home from the optometrist's office, and I was wearing my first set of prescription lenses. Dusk was falling, so I found myself looking out the car window at the moon. Awestruck by what I could now see, I continued to take my glasses off and put them on again. The difference was both glaring and astonishing. I had always known the moon existed because I wasn't completely blind, which basically meant I could identify the general location of that fuzzy glowing orb in the night sky. But never had I known how glorious the moon could be. The complexity of its cratered surface, the clarity of its circumference, the brilliance of the halos of light emanating from its center—revelations each. I was nothing short of transfixed.

Prior to that evening I had simply assumed everyone else saw the world in the same way that I did, which is to say, as blurry and nondescript. After all, the moon was simply too far away for anyone to see it with any sort of clarity. It wasn't until I was handed a set of corrective lenses that I realized just how much I had been missing and just how much more there was to see and understand. Before then, I was seeing only in the most technical sense. With my new lenses, however, I was able to make out far more detail, more depth, and more texture. Even though nothing had changed about my surroundings, everything had changed. It was as if a whole new world had opened up before me—one that I had inhabited my entire life but had never truly known, much less understood.

Of course, my story is by no means exceptional. Countless others suffer from some degree or kind of vision impairment, both literal and metaphorical. The apostle Paul said as much when he wrote to the church at Corinth that we all "see through a glass, darkly" (1 Cor. 13:12 KJV). According to Paul, we see (Greek: *blepomen*) through a reflective surface (*di esoptrou*) in an enigma (*en ainigmati*). In other words, life is incredibly complex and few things are clear. Nothing is straightforward or simple. It's almost as if, from the apostle's perspective, the whole of human life is one long attempt to make sense of a series of ancient, cryptic riddles presented in reverse image on a mirror made of hammered sheet metal. Or, to put a more modern spin on it, we're all like nearsighted kids trying to see and describe to one another the various intricacies of a glowing rock 238,900 miles away. Needless to say, that's no small task.

Centuries after Paul, the philosopher Hans-Georg Gadamer would suggest something similar. All humans, said Gadamer, interpret, understand, and, ultimately, come to know the world and their place in it from a "historically situated consciousness" (i.e., a particular sociohistorical location), which establishes the horizon beyond which they cannot see.[1] Following both Paul's and Gadamer's line of thinking, some emphasize the negative implications of this all-too-human reality, focusing on the ways that our vision is inherently limited, obscured, or otherwise clouded by the "darkness" of the "glass" through which we see. Indeed, our vision is often far more impaired than we realize. In the absence of corrective lenses, we remain blind to the true depth of our blindness.

Thus, for both Paul and Gadamer, there's no denying that we see through a glass, *darkly*. However, there is also no denying that we can still *see* through that glass, even if darkly. This somewhat more positive assessment of the human condition should not be mistaken for a naive optimism that would ignore or deny the very real consequences of sin. Rather, it reflects an understanding of the created order as fundamentally constituted by God's trinitarian relationality, a topic we will take up in greater detail in the following chapter. For now it is enough to say that, regardless of whether one emphasizes clarity or obscurity, the inescapable truth is that to be human is simply to envision the world through a particular set of lenses that are not merely "coloring" our view of the world but also making it possible. The opaque mirrors that provide us with an indirect awareness of reality are the very things that create the necessary conditions for any human knowledge at all. From this perspective, the problem is not so much that everything we know about reality is always already filtered in some form or fashion. That's just part of what it means to be a human being. Rather, the problem is that we so often fail to recognize that our vision is filtered through any kind of lens at all.

We humans are masters at convincing ourselves that our picture of the world corresponds directly to the way things really are—as if my localized perspective somehow provides me with a total or all-encompassing view of reality that holds true for everyone, everywhere, at all times. In other words, if the moon is blurry to me, then

---

1. Hans-Georg Gadamer, *Truth and Method* (New York: Continuum Books, 2004), xxi.

it must be blurry for everyone because, as we all know, moons are just blurry. On this point, students of psychology share something in common with their theological counterparts, for both traditions of inquiry are concerned, on the one hand, with exposing the various ways in which we are blind to our own blindness (on both conscious and unconscious levels) and, on the other hand, with developing a deeper, more penetrating insight into the human condition. In this way, both psychology and theology seek to develop constructive visions of life that will ultimately lead to human flourishing, but they also recognize that, in order to do so, we have to be honest about the ways in which our vision is at best, limited, and at worst, obscured.

To say that our vision is obscured is not to make a moral judgment. It is rather to say that, because we are all located somewhere, our vision is simply limited. No one has a view from nowhere. Again, that's just what it means to be human. At other times though, as the psychoanalytic tradition reminds us, we are willfully self-blinded. Making matters worse, we are also blinded by others on both interpersonal and societal levels. Still, regardless of the origins of our vision impairment, we have no chance of seeing clearly if we don't first acknowledge that each of us, in some form or fashion, needs our vision enhanced, expanded, and refined.

To move toward this kind of clarity of vision, students of psychology and theology must find a way to come to terms not only with *what* we see when we look upon the world but also with *how* we see. That is, we need a process that will enable us to see more clearly—a rigorous and reliable method that will be capable of expanding our field of view by drawing on a broader and more diverse set of resources and, at the very same time, refining our vision by allowing us to name and critically engage the various assumptions that (for good and for ill) inform and constrain our pictures of reality. Of course, a constructive theological method of this kind would be helpful for any person of faith hoping to see the world with a greater degree of clarity. However, just as a reminder, our primary concern in this book is not with Christians in general but with students of psychology in particular. Our chief aim is to equip them with a more robust set of tools and resources that will enable them to develop a

growing capacity for engaging in and reflecting on psychological topics, practices, and questions in ways that are theologically informed
(not to mention theologically interesting!).

To make this all a bit more concrete, consider the phoropter for a
moment (see fig. 1.1). Anyone who relies on vision correction knows
what a phoropter is, even if they have never heard the term. A phoropter is that medieval looking contraption an optometrist uses during eye exams. The goal of an eye exam is obvious: clarity of vision.
However, the method the optometrist uses to determine the correct
prescription for a person's contacts or eyeglasses is somewhat heuris-
tic. She cycles through a series of lenses, trying out various combinations, asking the patient to decide which lens allows them to see more
clearly: "Lens number one, or lens number two? Number three, or
number four?" It is a dynamic, iterative, discovery-oriented method
based on a good deal of trial and error. More importantly, though,
the goal of the process is not to find the one right lens that will deliver
20/20 vision, but rather to identify the unique combination of lenses
that will provide the clearest picture of the object in view. And this
kind of clarity emerges not by peering through a solitary lens but
through a convergence of multiple lenses.

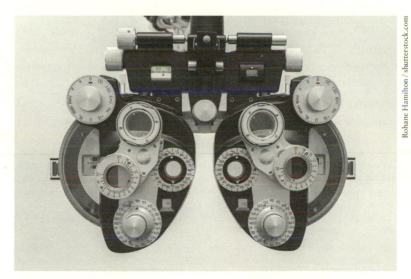

Rohane Hamilton / shutterstock.com

Figure 1.1. The phoropter

Focusing Our Vision

The phoropter serves as a helpful metaphor for thinking about theological method in general and its relationship to psychology more specifically, in large part because it dispels some of our misconceptions about what a method is and whether or not theology could ever be methodological.[2] You might think of theological method as somewhat analogous to what you would find in the methods section of an article published in a psychology journal, but with some very important qualifications. In the first place, as Bernard Lonergan rightly points out, "Method is not a set of rules to be followed meticulously by a dolt. It is a framework for collaborative creativity."[3] Rather than establishing a series of rigid steps designed to (re)produce a predetermined outcome, a theological method is a dynamic, creative, collaborative mode of reflection that seeks to generate insight (i.e., clarity of vision) by attending to a number of sources (i.e., lenses)—namely, the biblical text, a local worshiping community (often connected to a denomination), the historical theological tradition, one's personal experience, and the broader cultural context.

We will say more below regarding each of these normative sources, but for now it is enough to say that, as with a phoropter, the most helpful way to proceed is not to find a single, all-purpose lens that can deliver 20/20 vision, but instead to rotate through various combinations of lenses, paying special attention to points of convergence and divergence. Unfolding as it does in real time and in response to concrete, lived experiences, a method of this sort does not operate according to a set procedure; rather, it is an iterative process intended to generate cumulative and progressive insights.[4] While the goal of

2. We are not the first to suggest that the phoropter might be a helpful metaphor for theological reflection. See Caroline J. Simon, *Bringing Sex into Focus: The Quest for Sexual Integrity* (Downers Grove, IL: InterVarsity, 2012); and Robert K. Johnson, Craig Detweiler, and Kutter Callaway, *Deep Focus: Film and Theology in Dialogue* (Grand Rapids: Baker Academic, 2019).

3. Bernard Lonergan, *Method in Theology* (Toronto: University of Toronto Press, 1990), 1.

4. "A method is a normative pattern of recurrent and related operations yielding cumulative and progressive results. There is a method, then, where there are distinct operations, where each operation is related to the others, where the set of relations forms a pattern, where the pattern is described as the right way of doing the job,

the process is to gain clarity about the world in general, as a *theological* method, its more specific aim is to develop clarity regarding who God is, who we are as humans in relation to God, and, by extension, how we might participate in the presence and movement of God in the world.

Here, students of psychology will once again find themselves at home within the domain of theology, for neither psychologists nor theologians pursue deeper and more penetrating insights into the human condition simply for the sake of self-edification (although it can be personally quite edifying). In a very real sense, the whole project is simply dead on arrival if it fails to move in the direction of helping others. Much like optometrists making the most of a phoropter, theologians develop a method so that they might grow in wisdom themselves. But additionally, they seek to turn to others and ask, What if you looked at things through a different set of lenses? Which is clearer, lens number one or number two? Number three or number four?

Speaking less metaphorically and a bit more technically, what we are really talking about is developing a theological hermeneutic—a way of critically and appreciatively *seeing* and comprehending what might be called the "poetics" of life.[5] As a hermeneutic, it functions as a means for describing, interpreting, and understanding what humans make of the world (*poiēsis*) in which we live, move, and have our being. At the same time, it's an approach that allows room for (and sometimes demands) the reformulation of certain theological categories in light of our ever-changing contexts and in response to the data generated by fields of inquiry traditionally thought to be outside the domain of theology, such as psychology and the empirical sciences. In this respect, what we are describing in this chapter and will be demonstrating in subsequent chapters is not a static, linear procedure but a dynamic process for engaging in the practice of constructive theology that develops over time and in response to our on-the-ground experiences.

---

where operations in accord with the pattern may be repeated indefinitely, and where the fruits of such repetition are, not repetitious, but cumulative and progressive." Lonergan, *Method in Theology*, 4.

5. In terms of framing the theological task in this way, we are indebted to William Dyrness, *Poetic Theology: God and the Poetics of Everyday Life* (Grand Rapids: Eerdmans, 2011).

To be clear, we are proposing a constructive theological method because the focus of this book is on how students of psychology might go about doing theology as a lived practice.[6] It is therefore not an introduction to systematic theology, historical theology, or philosophical theology. We are not attempting to identify a single, coherent system of thought that can be traced throughout the various biblical, historical, and philosophical accounts. Neither is this necessarily a book on how to "integrate" theology and psychology, even if it might turn out to be helpful for those involved in integration efforts.[7] If anything, our approach to constructive theology precedes (and possibly supersedes) the integrative gesture by locating it within a larger interpretive framework. As biblical scholar and theologian Joel Green has suggested, given our account of the doctrine of creation (which we will describe more fully in the next chapter),

> Theology is an all-encompassing enterprise, so that subsequent segregation of science from theology could not mean that science would fall outside the purview of theology. Moreover, in so far as science is present as one of the sources for the theological enterprise, theology remains open

6. We are thus sympathetic to Miroslav Volf and Matthew Croasmun's definition of Christian constructive theology as "to discern, articulate, and commend visions of flourishing life in light of God's self-revelation in Jesus Christ." *For the Life of the World: Theology That Makes a Difference* (Grand Rapids: Brazos, 2019), 11.

7. An excellent example of how a constructive theological method precedes the integrative gesture can be found in Steven J. Sandage and Jeannine K. Brown, *Relational Integration of Psychology and Christian Theology: Theory, Research, and Practice* (New York: Routledge, 2018). Sandage and Brown advocate for a "relational" approach to the integration of theology and psychology, which not only takes place in particular contexts (and thus is not the only way to do integration) but also is inherently collaborative (i.e., it involves more than one scholar). Thus, for integration to be fully realized according to a relational model, both the theologian and the psychologist must come to the relationship not as incomplete halves but as whole human beings (and scholars) who form and (in)form one another in a dynamic of mutual reciprocity. Indeed, quoting Hal Foster, Sandage and Brown point out that "to be interdisciplinary you need to be disciplinary first" (*Relational Integration*, 90). In other words, "integration" assumes and, in an important respect, depends on the prior formation of the scholar/practitioner in a particular discipline, without which there would simply be nothing to integrate. Indeed, as we stated in the introduction, one of the principal contentions of this book is that we are not putting forward radically novel ideas but that we are simply theologians who are asking questions about how theology might inform psychological research and practice.

to the possibility of reformulation in relation to scientific discovery. . . . The question is not whether science will influence exegesis (or vice versa) since the two, science and religion, have interacted and continue to interact in a far more organic way than is typically acknowledged.[8]

As a consequence of this line of thinking, one of our operating assumptions is that students of psychology (and practitioners of psychology more broadly) need not become experts, for example, in the formulation of logical theorems or the historical development of theological doctrines. Rather, they first and foremost need a way of doing theology that allows them to put their theological know-how into practice. Because their primary task is to respond in life-giving ways to the infinitely complex, lived situations of other flesh-and-blood human beings, they are most in need of a dynamic, adaptable process that will provide them resources for elaborating on these concrete scenarios in ways that are necessarily creative and even improvisational, but no less clinically sound and theologically robust.

In certain respects, this is an imminently practical approach to theology. We are more concerned with developing a reliable set of strategies than we are with the tidiness of a particular syllogism or logical proof. This stands to reason because, much like therapy, constructive theology is anything but tidy. Both operate in realms that are inherently complex, which means that even if we could imagine the perfect set of doctrines that would make sense of each and every psychological construct, it would still be far from obvious which of these theological concepts apply in any given situation, much less how to apply them.

The challenge, then, is not how we might bring together two discrete intellectual disciplines, as if psychology (whether folk or professional) and the psychological sciences weren't always already forming and informing our theology. Nor is it how to apply ready-made theological doctrines to a concrete psychological problem (or vice versa). Our key concern is how students of psychology might respond faithfully to the world they inhabit from their own sociocultural context—a "respond-ability" that requires both keen insight and discernment. And for that, we need something more than systematic

8. Joel Green, *Body, Soul, and Human Life: The Nature of Humanity in the Bible* (Grand Rapids: Baker Academic, 2008), 24–25.

formulations and models of integration, however helpful they may be. Put a bit more simply, we need a holistic way of doing theology (i.e., a method) that generates a lived wisdom.[9]

Scientific Method and Theological Method

One of the difficulties we immediately encounter when it comes to describing this kind of constructive theological method for students of psychology is that, by and large, the word "method" means something quite different in psychological literature than it does in theological writing. Part of this confusion stems from the historical development of psychology, which originally started as a kind of philosophy of human thought, emotion, and behavior but eventually shifted more into the realm of the social sciences.[10] Many of the subdisciplines within contemporary psychology (e.g., cognitive science, psycho-analysis, psychology of religion) continue to hover in an ambiguous space between philosophy, the social sciences, and the natural sciences. Nevertheless, over the course of the past hundred years, practitioners of psychology as a whole have made a concerted effort to adopt the research methods and empirical tools of the "hard" sciences. As a

9. Indeed, it was in part her dissatisfaction with the available approaches to "integration" that prompted Megan Anna Neff to rethink both the purpose and value of using the language of "integration" as a practicing psychologist.

> Many of the traditional integration models and theories were built in the height of modernity, and therefore focused on abstracted theoretical models. As my classmates and I pondered what we were learning, one question kept swirling around in our conversations: "Yes, but what does this look like in the therapy room?" While we were learning important content, it didn't speak to the complexity we were witnessing or the "boots on the ground" questions we had about the practical nature of the clinical work we were learning to do. The class was successfully teaching us integration (theories and models), but it wasn't training us to *be integrators*. (Megan Anna Neff and Mark R. McMinn, *Embodying Integration: A Fresh Look at Christianity in the Therapy Room* [Downers Grove, IL: IVP Academic, 2020], 6–7, emphasis in original)

10. On this point, see Malcolm A. Jeeves and Thomas E. Ludwig, *Psychological Science and Christian Faith: Insights and Enrichments from Constructive Dialogue* (West Conshohocken, PA: Templeton Press, 2018). For those interested in how the historical development of psychology as a "science" has impacted contemporary integration efforts, see Kenneth I. Pargament's discussion in *Spiritually Integrated Psychotherapy: Understanding and Addressing the Sacred* (New York: Guilford Press, 2007).

result, the term "method" is most often deployed among psychologists to mean the linear, predictive, replicable techniques used to construct and empirically test scientific hypotheses (think again of the methods section in a psychology article published in a peer-reviewed journal). From this standpoint, a hypothesis may very well offer a compelling explanation of a given psychological phenomenon, but its primary value is that it generates accurate (i.e., mathematically significant) predictions about the observable world.

There are a number of ways to describe the scientific method, but for our purposes we can't do much better than the description we learned in kindergarten (see fig. 1.2). This basic, even elementary, understanding of "how to be a scientist" is not radically different

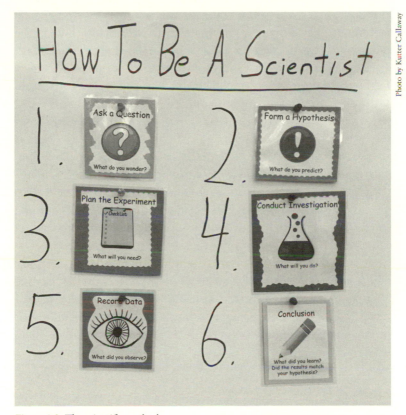

Figure 1.2. The scientific method

from the way we might describe "how to be a theologian." Indeed, the process by which one engages in scientific inquiry shares similarities with the process by which one engages in constructive theology. For instance, theological inquiries usually begin with an intractable question (about God, humans, and/or the world in which we live), and an initial prediction regarding how that question might be answered (i.e., a hypothesis). To explore this question, a plan is developed (experimental design), and a series of normative resources is consulted (conducting the investigation). Finally, observations are described, analyzed, and interpreted (recording data), and provisional conclusions are offered, which often include comments regarding limitations and possible directions for future research (conclusion).

These similarities notwithstanding, there are also important differences between the scientific method and what we mean by theological method. One key difference is that constructive theology locates the findings of scientific research within a larger theological framework. The insights generated by psychology are thus but one of a number of different data points from which the theologian draws. In truth, psychological scientists are only able to interpret and understand the data generated by their empirical research because they too operate within theoretical frameworks of some kind. Just as Thomas Kuhn suggested, all science takes place within a prevailing paradigm, which consists of a common (read: normative) set of theories, methods, goals, and even beliefs about the world.[11] The difference is that, whereas constructive theology makes the interpretive lenses guiding its explorations explicit, the natural sciences often elide (and sometimes altogether deny) their influence.

Put somewhat differently, both psychology and theology are inherently "traditioned" forms of inquiry, which simply means that anyone who operates within these traditions has inherited certain ways of understanding not only what they think their project is all about but also how to go about doing it.[12] Each of us is located somewhere

---

11. Thomas Kuhn, *The Structure of Scientific Revolutions* (Chicago: University of Chicago Press, 1962).

12. Brad Strawn, Ronald W. Wright, and Paul Jones, "Tradition-Based Integration: Illuminating the Stories and Practices That Shape Our Integrative Imagination," *Journal of Psychology and Christianity* 33, no. 4 (2014): 300–310.

(historically, socially, ethnically, culturally), and this basic situated-ness shapes not only how we see the world but also how we are related to what we see (i.e., the objects that come into our field of vision). Indeed, anyone engaged in the practice of theology and psychology would do well to come to a point where they are able to acknowledge that there is no such thing as an unfiltered, detached, or objective view "from nowhere."

As a consequence, identifying one's tradition and gaining clarity regarding its operative assumptions are critical parts of the constructive theological process. Whether a student of psychology or theology (or both), we always draw on other sources for making sense of empirical science, and perhaps more importantly, these sources function normatively and thus authoritatively, even if they go unnoticed. For example, clinical and research psychologists operate with implicit but often unacknowledged anthropologies (views of what it means to be human) and ontologies (views of what kind of "being" humans are) that inform, guide, and constrain their explorations of human thinking, feeling, and behavior. Even when they remain implicit, these perspectives regarding what it means to be human (and what a human is) determine not only which behaviors they find interesting but also how they gather and analyze their data and what they ultimately make of their research. By simply acknowledging these tradition-laden, embedded assumptions about human beings, we are able to critically examine them, explore how they are exerting pressure on our research projects, and revise, expand, or abandon them when necessary. In doing so, we also open our explorations to public scrutiny, which, in important respects, is actually a more as opposed to a less rigorous commitment to empirical methodologies.

A Process for Doing Constructive Theology

To describe theological method in this way is to identify at least two levels of discourse. Consider the phoropter again. On one level, it is helpful to step back and consider the device itself, inspecting the various lenses we are using, the overall sequence according to which we cycle through them, and even whether a given situation might call for an entirely different device. Second-order discourse of this kind is often called methodology, and it functions as a way of critically examining the apparatus itself—both the lenses through which we see the world and how they interact with one another. However, when we refer to a particular method for doing constructive theology, we are talking about what takes place when we use this device in the real world. On this level, rather than looking *at* a particular set of lenses and talking *about* them, we are looking *through* them.[13] What this means for students of psychology is that to do constructive theology is, at its most basic, to engage in the practice of cycling through a series of mutually clarifying lenses in pursuit of a deeper under-standing of human thought and behavior.

There is no single (or perfect) way of categorizing the various re-sources that are necessary for doing theology. Still, we can name at least five "lenses" that theologians in the (Protestant) Christian tradition have commonly peered through in order to gain clarity on their lives and the world: (1) the biblical text, (2) one's local worshiping community, (3) the historical theological tradition, (4) one's personal experience, and (5) the broader cultural context. It is important to keep in mind that this list is not organized according to any sort of hierarchy or preferred sequence. Each resource is critical in its own right, but there is no set procedure or starting point that dictates how we ought to cycle through these various lenses because, again, the key is to allow the insights from each domain to augment and clarify the others (see fig. 1.3).

Depending on the topic about which we are seeking clarity (e.g., social media), it might be best to start by reflecting on one's personal experience, one's cultural context, and how the discernment criteria of one's local church sheds light on the matter before moving to an (equally important) consideration of how the biblical text and the history of theological reflection inform, constrain, or otherwise guide these other perspectives.[14] It may even be helpful to experiment with some different sequences, considering the various insights that might

13. For a helpful introduction to this way of thinking about Christian theology, see Joshua Strahan, *The Basics of Christian Belief: Bible, Theology, and Life's Big Questions* (Grand Rapids: Baker Academic, 2020).
14. William Whitney and Carissa Dwiwardani expand on these ideas using an "Integration Quadrilateral" in their forthcoming book, *The Integration of Psychology and Christianity: A Student's Guide* (Downers Grove, IL: IVP Academic).

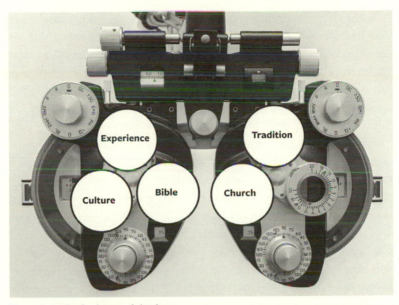

Figure 1.3. The five lenses of theology

emerge simply by choosing a new point of departure. Rather than determining beforehand where to begin or how the process will unfold, the key is to allow the unique focal point of each exploration (e.g., the spiritual and psychological *effects* of social media) to suggest and, in certain respects, determine where to start and how to proceed.

Speaking of social media, it is also the case that, while it is important to cycle through each lens at some point in the process, they are not always equally helpful. Augustine and Thomas Aquinas knew nothing of digital technologies, so even though these two stalwarts of the historic theological tradition offer keen insights into the human condition, they may not be the first or even primary source one consults in order to make theological sense of the social media habits of contemporary individuals. In this case, it is likely that we would be better served to draw primarily on the resources provided by our broader cultural context (e.g., media psychology) and to place those insights into a mutually enriching conversation with our local worshiping community, which is comprised of numerous other people of faith who are also attempting to navigate this media-saturated landscape with wisdom and discernment. To be clear, this is not to say that the Bible and the theological tradition are somehow unimportant or have nothing to say regarding contemporary phenomena like social media. It is rather to say that the ever-changing contexts we inhabit present a unique set of challenges that call for a mode of theological exploration that is equal parts nimble, creative, and adaptive.

For those who were hoping for more of a "plug-and-play" approach to theology, it might be more frustrating than fruitful to hear us repeatedly insist that all theological reflection is contextual and that every theological question comes with a unique set of demands. In the process of unpacking the various *mis*conceptions we all harbor about the nature and aims of theology, a certain amount of uneasiness is to be expected. But at a certain point, frustration can lead to disengagement, which would be the exact opposite of our desired outcome. So rather than continue responding to every question of "Where should we start?" with a cryptic "It depends," it's probably more helpful to point out that, based on our own experience, one of the most productive places to start is anywhere tension or dissonance can be found among the various theological resources.

At the risk of mixing our metaphors, Warren Brown has suggested something similar with his "resonance model." Brown, a neuropsychologist also engaged in constructive theological work, pictures the various sources of human knowledge as radios that broadcast signals with a particular frequency and wavelength, each of which has unique implications for our understanding of "truth."[15] The most reliable knowledge emerges at the point of convergence where the sound waves from various domains—namely science, rationality, experience, tradition, and Scripture—meet and overlap. For Brown, no single source or signal can be equated with the truth (not even Scripture). Nevertheless, our understanding of reality is enhanced and enriched when the signals in this acoustic field resonate with one another. Likewise, our understanding can become muddied when there is only dissonance.

15. Warren S. Brown, "Resonance: A Model for Relating Science, Psychology, and Faith," in *Integrating Psychology and Theology: Research and Reflections*, ed. Al Dueck (Pasadena: Fuller Seminary Press), 293–313.

Brown's is an aural rather than visual metaphor, but the implications are the same. In essence, to do theology is to seek a deeper
understanding of truth by engaging in a dynamic, iterative process
that brings together a multitude of epistemic sources. As such, a
certain amount of dissonance is not only to be expected but is gen-
erative. Returning to our visually oriented metaphor, these points
of tension are not hurdles to overcome but are rather opportunities
for generating insight. Indeed, as philosopher and ethicist Caroline
Simon has noted, "Orthodoxy is too often assumed to preclude multiplicity. If views are lenses, however, . . . multiplicity plus convergence
yields clarity."[16] In other words, the goal of the theological task is not
just about developing an ability to see the world (sight), it's about
seeing the world well (insight). And to see the world well—to gain
insight—we often need to look through a multitude of (sometimes
contrasting) lenses at one and the same time.

Our hope in describing this kind of approach to constructive theological inquiry is that it will resonate with a wide swath of Protestant
sensibilities. Nevertheless, it remains a profoundly traditioned approach to theology, which means that the process we are outlining
here might not reflect the same commitments and assumptions as the
tradition each of our readers has inherited.[17] Although we believe it
reflects how lived theology most often takes place on the ground,
some may be more comfortable with an established procedure—one
that, for example, always begins with an analysis of the biblical material and seeks to interpret personal experience, the wisdom of the
local church, the history of theological reflection, and the broader
culture in and through this singular lens. Karl Barth is well known
to have described his theological method in precisely this way: "Take
your Bible and take your newspaper, and read both. But interpret
newspapers from your Bible."[18] Using our terminology, Barth was
suggesting that a key resource for doing theology is indeed one's
broader cultural context (the newspaper). But for Barth, the Bible

16. Simon, *Bringing Sex into Focus*, 29.
17. Astute readers will recognize that we are describing a slightly modified version
of the Wesleyan Quadrilateral.
18. "Barth in Retirement," *Time*, May 31, 1963, http://content.time.com/time
/subscriber/article/0,33009,896838,00.html.

should always serve as the fixed "lens" through which everything else ought to be interpreted and understood.

In certain respects, we are of the same mind as Barth concerning the role of Scripture in theology. As theologians, we consider the Bible authoritative for Christian life and practice—essential for the task of doing theology. There may be instances in which the biblical text has very little to say about a given topic, but at no point are we simply free to dismiss it or disregard it. That is to say, *what the Bible means* will always be open to interpretation and up for debate, but *that the Bible matters* is not in question. Borrowing again from Alasdair MacIntyre, the Christian theological tradition is constituted by nothing other than our shared commitment to argue about what this authoritative text means.[19]

That being said, we are also suggesting that, at times, it is appropriate (and even advisable) to "reverse the hermeneutical flow" and interpret the biblical text in light of the newspaper.[20] Some, following Barth, might worry that to move in this direction is to undermine biblical authority or to subject it to the fickle winds of sociocultural change. But these fears are largely unfounded for two reasons. First, while it is always important to avoid reading into the biblical text that which is simply not there (i.e., eisegesis), the truth of the matter is that we have no other choice but to read Scripture from our situated standpoint—from the concrete, sociocultural context in which we are embedded. Yet, rather than being a problem to solve, this is simply part of what it means for the biblical text to function as authoritative Scripture for the people of God. We read the biblical text not as isolated individuals in a hermetically sealed chamber but as members of a particular community, located in a specific time and place, responding to concrete issues. There simply is no such thing as a "plain" reading of the text. Pretending as if there were risks a host of self-serving distortions rooted in a lack of self-awareness.

19. Alastair MacIntyre, *Whose Justice? Which Rationality?* (Notre Dame, IN: University of Notre Dame Press, 1988).

20. We have appropriated the phrase "reverse the hermeneutical flow" from Craig Detweiler and Barry Taylor, *A Matrix of Meanings: Finding God in Popular Culture* (Grand Rapids: Baker Academic, 2003), 319n5.

Second, given that the Bible stands at the heart of the constructive theological task, it is important to underscore that, in its function as Scripture, no interpretation of the biblical text takes place in the absence of the ongoing presence and activity of the Spirit of God. The same can be said of theological reflection more broadly. It is a fundamentally in-spirit-ed endeavor, which means that, whether we are interpreting the Bible from the newspaper or vice versa, the entire theological project hinges on the ongoing presence and activity of the Spirit of God who holds these various perspectives together in their creative tension. And just as we can be confident that the Spirit is at work in and through our reading of Scripture, so too can we be confident that, in conversation with our local worshiping community, the larger theological tradition, our personal experience, and the biblical text, the Spirit is also up to something in the broader culture.

A Cultural Lens

For the most part, the five lenses we have identified as normative resources for the theological task are fairly self-explanatory. As we endeavor not simply to know about God but to know God more deeply in our concrete lives, it is critical that we consider what the biblical text has to say (Bible), what our local worshiping community has discerned (church), how the historic theological tradition we have inherited navigated similar terrain (tradition), and the lived wisdom we have cultivated in our journey of discipleship (experience). For the sake of clarity, we have been talking about these resources as if they were distinct, but in truth they are always already interrelated, which means that a major element of the constructive theological process is simply being more critically aware of their constant interaction and, by extension, more intentional about how their various points of convergence and divergence might help us sharpen our vision.

Culture, the final lens, is likely the most fuzzy, both in terms of what it means and in terms of how it might serve as a theological resource. The primary reason is because, much like the word "method" (and "theology"!), the word "culture" often functions as an umbrella term that ends up being used in different ways by different people (even within the same discipline) depending on the context and the audience. For instance, the great majority of psychology students are exposed to the term "culture" as if it were entirely about racial and ethnic diversity. However, cultural psychologists Hazel Rose Markus and Alana Connor define culture much more broadly as "the ideas, institutions, and interactions that tell a group of people how to think, feel, and act."[21] Their definition reflects their primary goal as psychologists, which is not so much to understand culture per se, but how culture generates our sense of self, that is, our enculturated identity. Employing a slightly different definition, evolutionary biologist Robert Boyd suggests that culture is "the storehouse of gradually accumulated, local, and typically tacit knowledge."[22] On Boyd's view, culture is more than a mere set of ideas that humans pass on to one another; it is the evolutionary principle that has enabled humans to spread, adapt, and thrive in nearly every ecological niche on the planet.[23]

A distinct but related definition can be found in the work of neuroscientist Antonio Damasio: "Humans have distinguished themselves from all other beings by creating a spectacular collection of objects, practices, and ideas, collectively known as cultures. The collection includes the arts, philosophical inquiry, moral systems and religious beliefs, justice, governance, economic institutions, and technology and science."[24] Notably, Damasio's notion of culture shares certain similarities to Boyd's, and Marcus and Connor's. However, beyond the transmission of shared knowledge, culture for Damasio also includes the creation of material objects and systems of belief. Depending on one's perspective, this more expansive view of culture either complicates matters to such a degree that the word means nothing because it covers everything that humans do, or it makes culture a rich and fertile ground calling for exploration.

21. Hazel Rose Markus and Alana Conner, *Clash! How to Thrive in a Multicultural World* (New York: Plume, 2014), xix.

22. This quote is taken from Stephen Macedo, who wrote the introduction to Boyd's book and concisely summarizes Boyd's definition of culture. Robert Boyd, *A Different Kind of Animal: How Culture Transformed Our Species* (Princeton: Princeton University Press, 2018), 2.

23. Boyd, *Different Kind of Animal*, 21.

24. Antonio Damasio, *The Strange Order of Things: Life, Feeling, and the Making of Cultures* (New York: Pantheon, 2018), 1.

These complexities notwithstanding, because our aim is to incorporate "culture" into a larger theological project, our definition is, like Damasio's, somewhat broad. From a theological perspective, we can say that culture is "what humans make of God's creation."[25] It might strike some as a fairly straightforward definition, but a number of assumptions about the created order, human creativity, and divine agency are embedded within it. We will say more about these theological assumptions in the chapters to come, but for now it is enough to say that human culture-making assumes numerous forms. Each embodies a distinct set of features, yet shares a common thread, or "trace," with the others. Framed in this way, we can think of culture as something that is both tangible and intangible, both the concrete artifacts a society generates and the *volksgeist* (i.e., the spirit of the people) that animates these creative activities (we'll return to a discussion of how the Spirit of God relates to the spirit of people in chap. 3).

Whatever we call the common thread that ties together the various strands of a society's creative work, the primary point is that culture is embodied, expressed, and transmitted in and through a variety of forms that range from the concrete and particular to the abstract and general. Starting with the most concrete, we can think of human culture in terms of its material *products*—the various symbolic and technological artifacts it creates (e.g., tools, texts, works of art). But culture also finds expression in a constellation of *practices* (religious, aesthetic, political) that organize and orient our shared lives together, many of which incorporate (and give meaning to) the material artifacts we produce. These practices, in turn, serve as the lifeblood of numerous cultural *institutions*. The boundaries that distinguish institutions from the individuals that make up those institutions are often blurry, but generally speaking, institutions operate as both (1) a network of systems (technological, economic, legal) that organize our social landscape and determine how we ought to navigate our communal lives and (2) a series of underlying structures (political, ideological, mythological) that lend a sense of coherence to our collective activities, most often by providing us with robust narrative

25. We are indebted here to William A. Dyrness, *The Earth Is God's: A Theology of American Culture* (Maryknoll, NY: Orbis Books, 1997), xv.

resources for envisioning our culturally specific social arrangements as completely "natural"—that is, as a reflection not of our particular location but of the way things truly are.

By mentioning these deep structures, we are naming a more abstract dimension of culture. But that doesn't mean it has no bearing on everyday life. Rather, at this level of abstraction, culture begins to demonstrate a kind of non- or extra-human agency, exerting a top-down or whole-part influence that operates outside of human control and often without our consent. Indeed, it is only at this level of abstraction that we can speak reasonably about cultural *phenomena* (e.g., artistic trends, societal movements, political uprisings) and develop *theories* (whether philosophical, social-scientific, or critical) that explain these phenomena in terms of how they are causally associated with the construction of our *identities* (ethnic, linguistic, tribal, sexual).

Interestingly enough, the discipline of psychology is implicated in each of these cultural domains:

- *products* (research studies, journal articles, books)
- *practices* (clinical work, laboratory research, professional conference-going)
- *institutions* (universities, professional societies)
- *phenomena* (renewed nationalism, popularized cognitive behavioral techniques for weight loss)
- *theoretical frameworks* (psychodynamic, developmental, evolutionary)

Significantly, each of these aspects of psychology plays a part in the development of our sense of self and in our ability to come to a deeper understanding of our own intersecting *identities* as enculturated human beings.

As a result, the clinical methods, empirical tools, and theoretical frameworks of the psychological sciences are capable of providing Christians with much-needed insight into this thing we call "culture" (including the culture of psychology), especially as it concerns what it means to be a human inhabiting a particular culture, what it means for those humans to thrive in their own cultural context, and how we understand our role in helping other humans feel, think, and behave in ways that lead to their flourishing. Because it is a human project, psychology is far from perfect, but as one of numerous other lenses incorporated into the constructive theological task, it helps clarify our vision, granting us a depth of understanding regarding the human condition that would otherwise remain inaccessible.

On the Other Side of the Phoropter

Some may be slightly uncomfortable with our apparent willingness to place the findings of the psychological sciences into a mutually enriching dialogue with the historic theological tradition or, perhaps even more distressingly, the biblical text. We will not be able to dispel these concerns in their entirety, but we do hope to show that it is for expressly theological reasons that we are able to identify psychology as a trustworthy (and even authoritative) source that can inform and guide our understanding of who God is and who we are as human beings. In fact, as the next chapter discusses in greater detail, it is creation's trinitarian structure that underwrites our ability to endorse what we discover about the world through psychology (or any science, for that matter). Likewise, in chapter 3 we consider how a robust pneumatology (i.e., our view of the Spirit) encourages us to approach culture with the expectation that we will encounter God already at work in people's lives. Finally, chapter 4 considers the incarnation as the key theological doctrine animating our approach to positive psychology and its vision of human flourishing.

Still, questions will inevitably remain. Which of the various lenses has the final word? When, where, and how does contemporary psychology function authoritatively, and what are its limits? How do we know whether our personal experience is blinding us to what Scripture says or granting us much-needed insight into an aspect of the biblical text that would otherwise go unseen and unnoticed? None of these questions are easily addressed, and in certain respects, that is exactly the point. At the risk of overstatement, constructive theology is rarely if ever concerned about questions that are straightforward or simple because life is almost never straightforward or simple. If it were, then wisdom and discernment would not be required. We would simply do what is obvious. In the real world, though, things are far more complex, which is why theology takes practice and develops over time. It's not simply a way of thinking but is rather an ongoing process in which one returns time and again to a handful of intractable questions, asking them in new ways and in light of new contexts, refusing to soften their critical edge by pretending they could ever be easily resolved. Its chief aim is not the production of "knowledge" per se, but the development of our capacity to navigate the complexities of life in robust and faithful ways. And just like any other lived practice, the more we do it, the more it becomes a part of our body's habituated, unconscious, reflexive response to what we encounter in the various niches we inhabit.

Speaking of the body, the role of the larger community (i.e., the body of Christ) in developing these theological competencies cannot be overstated. The fundamentally communal nature of the theological task is especially salient for students of psychology because they are learning not only how to see themselves and their surroundings more clearly but also how to help others do the same. In other words, there is no sense in which their growing capacity for doing theology begins or ends with them alone. The same is true for every person of faith. But given their calling to enter a helping profession, students of psychology are preparing for a future in which they will be located on the other side of the metaphorical phoropter. One of their primary tasks in their role as psychological practitioners will be to help their clients see the world more clearly by having them look at themselves and the world around them from a variety of different perspectives and asking the question: Which is clearer? Number one or number two? Number three or number four?

The challenge, of course, is to do this while acknowledging that none of us have 20/20 vision ourselves. In some ways we are the blind leading the blind. Which is why, before responding, it is imperative that clinicians not only listen to their clients as they describe the way each lens sharpens or blurs their vision but also that they listen well. Just because the moon appears to us like a fuzzy glowing orb doesn't mean that it looks the same to everyone else. In other words, there is no such thing as a one-size-fits-all set of prescription lenses, in large part because no one's vision is impaired in exactly the same way. And just as it is with physical sight, so it is with theological insight. Clarity of vision isn't about seeing what can already be seen, just with more depth and detail. Rather, it's about peering in and through the world that can be seen in order to come into the presence of what cannot be seen. After all, as Paul reminds us, "what is seen is temporary, but what is unseen is eternal" (2 Cor. 4:18 NIV).

Questions for Reflection and Discussion

1. How would you describe your current theological method—the process by which you make sense of your life and the world as a Christian?

2. What are the risks of the approach to constructive theology we have outlined?

3. What does "culture" mean to you theologically? Psychologically? Why does it matter how you answer these questions?

4. In what ways does psychology currently serve as a resource for you as you engage the world theologically?

Resources for Reading and Exploration

Neff, Megan Anna, and Mark R. McMinn. *Embodying Integration: A Fresh Look at Christianity in the Therapy Room*. Downers Grove, IL: IVP Academic, 2020.

Veeneman, Mary. *Introducing Theological Method: A Survey of Contemporary Theologians and Approaches*. Grand Rapids: Baker Academic, 2017.

Volf, Miroslav, and Matthew Croasmun. *For the Life of the World: Theology That Makes a Difference*. Grand Rapids: Brazos, 2019.

2

Creation as a Trinitarian Project

Key takeaways from this chapter:

- The doctrine of creation provides the framework for theological reflection on psychology.
- God has created a world that can be explored and investigated.
- The investigation and exploration of the created world by humans is one of the ways that psychology can be understood from a theological perspective.

Having its start in the 1940s, IKEA has grown from humble business beginnings, where it originally sold things like pens and wallets, into a superstore with locations all over the world. IKEA is primarily

Portions of this chapter have been adapted from William Whitney, "Beginnings: Why the Doctrine of Creation Matters for the Integration of Psychology and Christianity," *Journal of Psychology and Theology* 48, no. 1 (2020): 44–65, https://doi.org/10.1177/0091647119837024.

known for its affordable, flat-packed furniture and maze-like stores. You can go into IKEA needing to quickly grab a lamp, only to leave six hours later with a hot dog in hand for dinner, a dresser, and a date for Saturday night with someone you met in the bookshelf section while trying to pronounce "Hemnes." It is truly a special place. And, if you've ever wondered where those names for IKEA products come from, as I (William) have, they are named after geographic areas of Norway, Sweden, or Denmark. For instance, beds are often named for regions in Norway, sofa names bear a resemblance to towns in Sweden, rugs derive their nomenclature from areas in Denmark or Sweden, while other products are Scandinavian women's and men's names.[1]

My wife, Kim, is particularly talented at putting together IKEA furniture. She has a system that has never failed yet—a skill forged out of sheer necessity while a college student. Plus, she is exceptionally good at following directions, which I have struggled with since I was a child. First, she opens the box and finds the directions. Then she organizes all the pieces according to the different steps. Next, she opens all the plastic bags with the screws, nuts, bolts, pegs, and other items (I'm sure these other items have names, but I've never seen anything like them before). She lays out every single one of these pieces in its entirety first and organizes them by their numbers (if they have them). That way, even if the connection pieces look similar, she knows exactly which ones are which according to the numbers.

The next step she takes is to create the framework of the piece of furniture, which is the first step in the instructions. This, as she'll tell you, is one of the most important parts of the job. She'll also tell you to be patient and not skip to the end, because if you don't get the framework part of the assembly correct the other parts won't fit right. Once she is confident that the framework is put together properly, she goes ahead and moves forward by beginning slowly, step by step, to attach the other pieces.

1. Morgan Cutolo, "How IKEA Products Get Their Crazy-Sounding Names," *Reader's Digest*, Dec. 28, 2017, https://www.rd.com/article/ikea-product-names; Sarah Wyman, "Ikea's Furniture Names Are Famous for Being Hard to Pronounce, but They Aren't Completely Random. Here's Where They Come From," *Business Insider*, Aug. 23, 2018, https://www.businessinsider.com/ikea-furniture-names-origin-story-2018-8.

As can be seen with IKEA furniture, frameworks are important because they provide the base that supports everything else. If you want to get that dresser or bookshelf to look right and to sit flush with the wall, then it's important to pay close attention to getting the framework correct before you move on. You can think of this chapter on creation as the framework that supports a lot of other theological doctrines for interdisciplinary work between theology and psychology. The details will become more clear in this chapter, but, in short, the triune God's ordering of the world and ongoing relationship with it is the framework that makes inquiry into the world through science and psychology possible.

As mentioned in our previous chapter, one of the key goals of this book is to help you as a psychology student to develop a greater awareness of and competency with Christian theology. We are most interested in helping you develop a greater depth of theological skill and reflection regarding psychology and psychological subdisciplines. While the majority of our students come to us already interested in theological reflection on the discipline of psychology, the common question they often ask is, Where do I begin? This question is important because, just like IKEA furniture, our beginning theological reflections are a question about getting the framework right. In answer to that question, we suggest that the basic place to begin our theological reflection is within the framework of a trinitarian account of God's relations with the world.

God as Trinity (Father, Son, and Spirit) is not some sort of abstract principle or speculative theory but a serious reflection on God's mission in the world through the Son and Spirit to bring wholeness and healing to the created order. To make it more personal, when we begin with a trinitarian account of God's relations with the world, we are also engaging in serious consideration of what it means for us as the community of Christ to be a part of God's mission and vision.

God's self-disclosure through the Son and Spirit in the created world is the foundation, blueprint, or framework for how we can begin to understand the backdrop to our own embodied lives. The revealing of God's self as trinitarian is an important part of this framework for providing a vision for how our lives are transformed through the person and work of Christ. The mission and vision of

God have an ultimate end or aim (Greek: *telos*), which is to sustain, redeem, and bring wholeness to humanity—and the entire creation. As will become clear, our understanding of at least some of the features that characterize this healing and wholeness can be guided by the discipline of psychology. So, while we begin with the doctrine of the Trinity, this chapter will argue that a trinitarian account of creation and revelation sets the stage for how truths about the world can be discovered through the discipline of psychology specifically and science generally, and how knowledge about the world is discovered through human interaction with the physical realm.

Understanding more about the doctrines of creation and revelation is directly related to the question of how we can learn anything at all from the human sciences. The doctrines of both creation and revelation impact our theological reflection about psychology, and yet, they are doctrines that are often neglected by psychologists. That the doctrines of creation and revelation have been overlooked within psychology has not been intentional. It is simply that other doctrines, such as those pertaining to theological anthropology and the doctrine of sin, have oftentimes received more attention. The primary theological doctrine that continues to be the focus in psychology is the conception of the *imago Dei* (image of God),[2] and much of the time that the *imago Dei* is invoked, the discussion leans toward the negative aspects of humanity related to sin.[3] A focus on the *imago Dei* and sin makes sense considering that psychology specifically studies human thought and behavior, and often focuses on "abnormal" behavior or psychopathology.[4] However, out of all the Christian doctrines that are discussed in this book, the Christian doctrines of creation and revelation provide some of the most critical theological resources that enable us to have a more in-depth understanding of clinical work and research within the field of psychology.

2. Keith A. Puffer, "Essential Biblical Assumptions about Human Nature: A Modest Proposal," *Journal of Psychology and Christianity* 26, no. 1 (2007): 45–56.

3. David N. Entwistle and Stephen K. Moroney, "Integrative Perspectives on Human Flourishing: The *Imago Dei* and Positive Psychology," *Journal of Psychology and Theology* 39, no. 4 (2011): 295–303.

4. Such is the common argument put forward by several authors in Corey L. M. Keyes and Jonathan Haidt, eds., *Flourishing: Positive Psychology and the Life Well-Lived* (Washington, DC: American Psychological Association, 2003).

Creation and Revelation

When we speak of creation and revelation, we are talking about two related but different Christian doctrines. For understanding the term "revelation," we are talking about how God reveals God's own self through the Son and Spirit. When we use the term "creation" within Christian theology, this concept is a bit trickier, since the majority of students understand creation to refer to the Genesis narrative and how God created the world in the beginning. While it is true that the doctrine of creation does describe the beginnings of human and nonhuman life in Genesis, for our purposes here, we must also think of the Christian doctrine of creation as being a unifying theme that operates throughout Scripture and describes God's initial and ongoing relationship with the world.[5] The doctrine of creation does form the framework for understanding God's triune action through the Son and Spirit in the created world since its inception. However, in addition to this, the doctrine of creation is part of the larger Christian narrative that envisions the created world as the stage on which God acts to create new things through the redeeming and sanctifying work of Christ.[6] Consequently, when we talk about a trinitarian account of creation, we are saying something about how the triune God created in the beginning and continues to provide for both human and nonhuman life (like animals and plants) today. But in our understanding of the doctrine, it also says something about the ways that God reveals God's own identity within Christ and the Spirit.

By framing things in this way, several related theological topics rise to the surface that call for further exploration. A trinitarian account of creation does the following:

- Encompasses other doctrines like providence and common grace (terms we will return to later), both of which acknowledge that God continues to uphold, care for, and sustain the world
- Helps us understand how humans have a role in tending, keeping, and stewarding the earth through all kinds of activities, both aesthetic and scientific in nature

5. Pamela Ebstyne King and William B. Whitney, "What's the 'Positive' in Positive Psychology? Teleological Considerations Based on Creation and *Imago* Doctrines," *Journal of Psychology and Theology* 43, no. 1 (2015): 47–59.

6. King and Whitney, "What's the 'Positive' in Positive Psychology?," 47.

- Upholds the goodness of creation and the human creature, and maintains that the exploration of God's creation through the sciences or psychological science is a worthy endeavor
- Offers a corrective to the physicalism or naturalism found within some streams of psychology that reduces humanity to a series of behavioral or neurological processes
- Provides a vision for how creation one day will be made whole and encompass a new heaven and a new earth (Rev. 21:1)

In sum, the created world is the stage where we experience the triune God's continuous and loving action of sustaining the world that has been created, redeeming fallen humanity, and ultimately bringing about the restoration of the entire created realm.[7] The world that God has created is able to be known; it is a world that can be explored and investigated, and this investigation and exploration are ways that psychology can be understood, at least from a theological perspective.

The rest of this chapter lays out how you might develop your theological skills pertaining to the doctrines of creation and revelation, and why these theological topics make a difference in your practice, study, and research for psychology. The aim is to help you more fully understand and explain (from a theological perspective) why psychology is a worthwhile endeavor by developing a greater awareness of and competency with a trinitarian understanding of creation. But perhaps even more important, our hope is that, as we discuss creation, you will begin to reflect on the lived wisdom of how God interacts with the world and human creatures and, in doing so, walk away changed—inspired by a vision for how God might want you to pursue your calling within the discipline of psychology.

Investigation into the Natural World and Human Nature

As authors who deeply believe in the benefit of engaging both psychology and Christian theology in conversation, we understand that there are some Christians who might not share our enthusiastic en-

7. King and Whitney, "What's the 'Positive' in Positive Psychology?," 48.

gagement with these two disciplines. Two possible reasons for these difficulties are that some Christians have either not reflected on how God might be present and active in the world at large or they hold religious and theological beliefs that make no room for God to be at work in the wider culture outside of the church. As a result, many Christians do not have an in-depth vision for how God's work in the world can incorporate discoveries in the sciences (even though these same Christians still go to the doctor and believe what their doctor says based on medical science). To counter such misconceptions, we find that a trinitarian understanding of creation provides the framework for how God allows elements of truth to be discovered in the world through the psychological sciences. However, we must acknowledge that some hesitations regarding psychology are well founded, and we should address them before moving on.

To begin, many areas of psychology operate with what we might call a *methodological naturalism*. Naturalism (at least in regard to the study of human thought and behavior) is the belief that what we can know about the human person can be explained through natural causes, and science can ultimately and fully explain the cognitive, emotional, and biological elements of human nature. Forms of naturalism also reduce the created realm of both human and non-human life to only biological, cognitive, and environmental causes and processes, and do not acknowledge any nonmaterial realities. *Physicalism* is a related term, and it describes a view of the human person as simply a sum of physical properties. *Scientism*, another associated concept, involves the belief that all things ultimately can be explained through science or scientific investigations of the natural world. According to scientism, if something cannot be explained scientifically, then it is simply because we don't have the scientific understanding yet to explain it. Scientism as a viewpoint will advocate that everything we observe in the world ultimately has a natural or biological root for the phenomena that we are observing that can be explained through science.[8]

8. Philosophers make the distinction between "epistemological naturalism" and "metaphysical naturalism." For the sake of our general overview, we have described both under the term "naturalism." For the nuances, see D. Gene Witmer, "Physicalism and Metaphysical Naturalism," Oxford Bibliographies, March 30, 2015, https://www

All these viewpoints ultimately have consequences for how we understand both the world and the human person, which is why we need to understand how they are functioning. More specifically, these views have implications for understanding things like moral behavior and epistemology (how we know what we know) in addition to ontology (the nature of being). Methodological naturalism within psychological research simply means that in the normal scientific method used in psychology, the supernatural or spiritual are bracketed out in order to find causal or correlational mechanisms.

Naturalism and *physicalism* are probably viewpoints that you are already familiar with, even if the terminology might be new, since they operate in the background of many views that are expressed either explicitly or implicitly within the natural or human sciences. For instance, in his work *What I Believe*, the British philosopher Bertrand Russell famously stated, "When I die I shall rot, and nothing of my ego will survive."[9] Sigmund Freud, in a similar way, operated with a naturalistic view of the human person that reduced conceptions of God to natural unconscious processes of the mind that were a way for humans to find safety in a father figure. Of course, this does not mean that Russell's and Freud's work can be characterized only in this way or that we cannot appreciate other aspects of their contributions to intellectual history. However, they do provide prominent examples of how both naturalist and/or physicalist understandings of the human person implicitly or explicitly operate in the background of many accounts of humanity from both psychology and philosophy.

Even if views of the human person are not explicitly stated as clearly as Russell's or Freud's, we must admit that psychology *does operate* with a functional or methodological naturalism. That is, psychologists are interested in understanding phenomena that fall within the realm of the natural and scientific, and thus bracket out any other kind of nonmaterial or supernatural causes.[10] This is perfectly normal

---

.oxfordbibliographies.com/view/document/obo-9780195396577/obo-9780195396577
-0258.xml.

9. Bertrand Russell, *Basic Writings of Bertrand Russell, 1903–1959*, ed. Robert E. Egner and Lester E. Denonn (New York: Routledge, 1992), 370.

10. Peter Hampson, "Theology and Psychology," in *Christianity and the Disciplines: The Transformation of the University*, ed. Oliver Crisp, Gavin D'Costa, Mervyn Davies, and Peter Hampson (London: Bloomsbury, 2014), 119.

and is the very nature of the scientific method that we discussed in chapter 1. However, even while operating within the bounds of the scientific method, psychology and other sciences are sometimes portrayed as providing a total and complete picture of human thought, behavior, and emotion—an understanding of the human that can be explained by psychology or science alone. Nevertheless, as Peter Hampson points out, even though this implicit (or sometimes explicit) methodological naturalism does occur within psychology, it does not follow that psychology can tell us everything we need or want to know about human nature. Said another way, psychology's methodological naturalism does not mean that, as Christians, we must subscribe to a comprehensive portrait of human nature that is solely naturalistic.[11]

Consequently, we must acknowledge that psychological research does at times seem to offer a portrait of human nature that operates with this kind of methodological naturalism. However, as Christians, because we believe that psychology alone cannot give a complete and comprehensive picture for human existence (ontology), we should not reduce the human creature to biological, cognitive, or emotional processes, as the assumption of naturalism in psychological research sometimes implies. Although we do not deny the reality of these natural processes and, for the most part, uphold psychological research that explains and gives insight into these processes, as Christians we believe that these processes were created by God and are sustained by God's life-giving Spirit. Keep in mind that psychological science is limited to those things that can be measured and observed within the natural realm, and while it offers valuable insights, it cannot provide a complete ontology for the ultimate goal or telos of humanity in the same way the Christian theological tradition can. For the Christian who studies psychology, what Scripture says about the human person and God's interaction with humanity provides the fundamental ontology (or primary lens) through which we understand the nature and purpose of humanity.

Christian Scripture identifies a goal or purpose for humanity and, in doing so, provides an orientation toward human personhood for Christian psychologists—whether or not it is specified or explained

11. Hampson, "Theology and Psychology," in *Christianity and the Disciplines*, 120.

through their psychological research or clinical practice. Psychologists who are also people of Christian faith thus seek to clarify what God intends for the human creature and to discern how the discipline of psychology might help illuminate these intentions. A trinitarian understanding of creation informs how one might understand the human person in ways that don't necessarily have to contradict psychological study but, in certain key instances, do remain outside the realm of psychological inquiry.

For instance, psychologists might give us many reasons why we should study human nature. Some of these reasons might include things like improving the quality of human life and ensuring proper development of infants, children, adolescents, and adults. Some psychologists might say they study human nature simply because human behavior is fascinating and worthy of investigation. All these reasons are well and good, and as Christians we agree to a certain degree. However, for the Christian who studies psychology, these reasons for exploring human thought and behavior are not the only reasons why we should engage in psychological study. As Christians, we also believe a fundamental starting point for the study of the human person is the ultimate value and worth of humanity. Theologically speaking, the human creature is granted dignity and worth because humans are created by the triune God who loves and cares for creation and who redeems creation through Jesus Christ.

This would be an example of how we might understand our study within psychology to be *deepened* and *broadened* by our Christian beliefs and values.[12] God's trinitarian action through Christ and the Spirit in relation to the human creature is also an example of how the Christian faith offers a "lived wisdom" that we talked about in chapter 1. Our beliefs and values about humanity and God are not just intellectual processes but are also embodied in an ethic (concrete actions) that moves us to respect human life and to live out this love for God and others through our studies within psychology.

Some might still wonder whether it really does matter for our studies within psychology that we operate with an underlying Christian

---

12. William Whitney and Carissa Dwiwardani, *A Student's Guide to Psychology and Christianity* (Downers Grove, IL: InterVarsity, forthcoming).

ontology that values the dignity and worth of humanity. In short, the answer is yes, it does. In fact, it matters ultimately. Whether you are pursuing a future in clinical or research psychology (or both), the dignity and worth of humans is rooted in a theology of creation. The value and worth of humanity outlined by a trinitarian account of creation also empowers us to be justice-oriented in how we speak up for the least of these (see Matt. 25:40–45) through our research and clinical practice within psychology.

Creation as a Framework for Understanding Psychological Science

Scripture gives us a clear vision of God ultimately moving and working in the world around us. In addition, it tells story after story of God inviting the community of Christ-followers (the church) to carry out God's work in the world. However, the biblical witness also indicates that humans are capable of knowing truths about the world that aren't necessarily found in the canon of Scripture. As counterintuitive as that might sound, Christian theologians have thought long and hard about this topic, and their deliberations are quite helpful. Some of the ideas about how we can know truths about the world that God makes available are through general and special revelation, providence, and common grace.

General and Special Revelation

Theologians use the term "general revelation" to acknowledge that God discloses God's own self in the world, and at least some of this disclosure is evident in creation through nature. This general revelation of God does not necessarily provide or lead humanity to salvation, but it does mean that if God created the world, then we can expect to see God's handiwork displayed in the very things that God has created. There are some well-known Scriptures that illustrate this sort of evidence; for example, "The heavens declare the glory of God; the skies proclaim the work of his hands" (Ps. 19:1 NIV) and "For since the creation of the world God's invisible qualities— his eternal power and divine nature—have been clearly seen, being understood from what has been made, so that people are without excuse" (Rom. 1:20 NIV).

These passages demonstrate that at least some aspects of God are seen in creation. Even in the beginning chapters of Genesis, God promises to be faithful to all creation and sustain it through the seasons and harvest (Gen. 8:21–23), thus establishing a general covenant of care for the world (this is the basis of the doctrine of providence). What we learn from general revelation is that God's relationship with the world continues unabated, and aspects of God's beauty, brilliance, wisdom, and order remain established for anyone to see in and through their observations of the created order. Some people might look at nature and see it only as a result of natural processes, but as Christians, we understand that there is a God behind those natural processes, and we often are moved with gratitude to God for the beautiful features of the natural world.

Special revelation similarly talks about God's self-disclosure and acknowledges that God is uniquely revealed in the person and work of Jesus Christ and in the continuing work of the Spirit. Special revelation also speaks to how the Spirit works through Scripture to help people understand the person and work of Jesus Christ. For those who grew up in some tradition of the Christian faith, special revelation is probably the more familiar of the two terms, especially insofar as it concerns the salvation and redemption made available through the life, death, and resurrection of Jesus.

Theologians over time have talked about the "two books" of knowledge given by God. The first book is generally thought to be creation, whereas the second book is Scripture. In 1615 Galileo argued that these two books cannot contradict each other, for they both represent God's communication to us.[13] Oxford theologian and scientist Alister McGrath similarly insists that the doctrine of creation represents a unified understanding of knowledge and God's communication with us.[14] What this means is that the created realm and Scripture represent two related ways that one can know God,

13. Richard J. Blackwell, *Galileo, Bellarmine and the Bible* (Notre Dame: University of Notre Dame Press, 1991), 20–22.

14. Alister McGrath, *A Scientific Theology* (Grand Rapids: Eerdmans, 2009), 1:257.

with Scripture embodying a more full and clear knowledge about God. For McGrath, there are not two different types of knowledge about God, one derived through general revelation and one through special revelation; rather, they are complementary modes of communication by the same divine reality. Thus, our approach, which is similar to McGrath's and those of numerous other theologians who have come before us, is to assume that if God made the world, then it makes sense that aspects of God's order, creativity, and life would be found in the created realm.[15]

One of the most basic foundations for engaging in theologically informed psychology is a unitary approach to knowledge that allows for certain truths to be gleaned from psychology. This does not mean that nature, the sciences in general, or psychology in particular give us specific or special knowledge of Jesus Christ that leads to redemption. However, it *does mean* that aspects of God's order, creativity, and wisdom are disclosed in the basic building blocks of the world. These indicators of who God is and how God operates can be discovered by those who inquire. What is more, God's very self—God's presence—can be encountered in and through our exploration of the world God created. Indeed, it is possible to discover these things about God through psychological and clinical science because, ultimately, God made it so.

Simon Oliver notes: "Genesis asks about the meaning of creation. It begins with the same realization upon which the edifice of science is built: the idea that the cosmos is ordered and rational in such a way that we can make sense of it, not from some external objective standpoint but from within the cosmos itself. We will see that Genesis adds another crucial claim, which is more alien to our scientific culture: creation is rational precisely because it is good."[16] Because God has fashioned the world in a certain kind of way, with a certain kind of physical reality that is knowable, these realities can be discovered through rigorous scientific investigation (both the natural and behavioral sciences).

15. Joel Green, *Body, Soul, and Human Life: The Nature of Humanity in the Bible* (Grand Rapids: Baker Academic, 2008), 257.
16. Simon Oliver, *Creation: A Guide for the Perplexed* (London: Bloomsbury, 2017), 8.

T. F. Torrance argues that nature may be "interpreted as pointing intelligibly beyond itself to God," but creation does not "permit any necessary inferences from its contingence to God."[17] This simply means that while aspects of creation (and the human person) are knowable through scientific investigation, the physical world can only speak about God in general terms and does not provide explicit knowledge of the life, death, and resurrection of Christ.[18] God did not have to make a world that would disclose something of its order to those who investigated it, but chose to graciously create a world that humans could interact with, and, in some way, come to understand through exploration. For Christians who study psychology, there are truths that can be discovered about the thoughts, feelings, and behaviors of human beings through clinical practice and psychological science. While these truths from psychology illuminate aspects of the wonder and complexity of human personhood, this knowledge does not provide a full-bodied understanding of the person and work of Christ. However, these truths should not be discounted or disregarded as lacking in value. In fact, it is just the opposite.

In summary, and from a theological perspective, God reveals aspects of who God is through the natural realm and Scripture. While these aspects of nature and Scripture are related, special revelation is clearer and more distinct than general revelation in the way that it speaks specifically to the work of Christ. However, general revelation concerns God's creation of, sustenance of, and ordering of the world. And while this order is complex, through exploration and careful observation we are able to learn about this world and the human person. The investigation of God's created realm can take many forms. We can explore it through travel, literature, art and music, and the sciences. Likewise, by drawing on the natural sciences or the social sciences, we can investigate the beautiful complexity of the world God has created.

Parents get a lot of joy watching their children explore and play on a playground or newly discovered beach. Children immerse them-

17. Thomas F. Torrance, *Space, Time, and Incarnation* (Edinburgh: T&T Clark, 1997), 62.
18. Thomas F. Torrance, *Reality and Evangelical Theology: The Realism of Christian Revelation* (Downers Grove, IL: InterVarsity, 1999), 12–13.

selves in their surroundings while examining every nook and cranny of their environment—finding features that adults will often miss. In the same way, we can assume that it brings God great delight to watch humans explore the vast playground of nature through the sciences and arts. Here is what Dallas Willard suggests: "God leads a very interesting life and is full of joy. . . . Undoubtedly he is the most joyous being in the universe. . . . We pay a lot of money to get a tank with a few tropical fish in it . . . but God has seas full of them which he constantly enjoys."[19]

Psychology is just one form that the delight-full exploration of God's world can take. The thoughts, behaviors, and feelings of humans are certainly complex. An argument could be made that, even when compared to what we know and do not know about the physical laws that govern the universe, human psychology is one of the most perplexing and uncharted terrains that scientists are attempting to understand. However, as Christians, we believe that, because God created the world with a certain order to it, investigation into human thoughts, feelings, and behaviors can and does yield results that will help us understand humanity. God created humans to be curious about creation (and one another). Through cultural tools of investigation that humans have also discovered, we can explore the physical realm through disciplines like physics and biology and continue to learn about the human person through disciplines like psychology and sociology. God has made creation in such a way that it will "disclose" its secrets to the one who inquires, which means that creation may be investigated and explored through the sciences in general and psychology in particular.[20]

Returning to our opening metaphor, you'll recall that the instructions for putting together a piece of IKEA furniture usually begin with a picture of what the final product looks like. This picture of the final product is important, since it gives you an idea of what things should look like and the goal you are striving to reach. So, while the framework is the doctrine of creation, it is vital to remember that theological reflection with psychology and theology has a purpose or

19. Dallas Willard, *The Divine Conspiracy: Rediscovering Our Hidden Life in God* (New York: HarperCollins, 1998), 62–63.
20. Torrance, *Space, Time, and Incarnation*, 2.

end goal. Moreover, as Christians studying psychology, our work has a greater purpose or end goal (*telos*) beyond just amassing information about human thought and behavior—or honing our research skills in order to get a job. The aim of becoming a practitioner of psychology is not simply to have a career or because we are enamored with the idea of seeing letters after our name (e.g., PhD, PsyD, MFT, MSW, LPC). Hopefully, as Christians, we are pursuing psychology as part of our vocational calling to align ourselves with God's mission in the world to bring justice, wholeness, and peace to those we come into contact with, through either our research or clinical practice.

As Megan Neff and Mark McMinn have pointed out, God by nature is missional and is at work "mending and tending" the universe.[21] Moreover, as the church, and as Christians who study psychology, we are invited to participate in the missional nature of the triune God through our vocation within psychology.[22] As a consequence, we can align ourselves with some of the missional activities of God through our work within one of the subdisciplines of psychology, especially given the fact that so much of the work we do within psychology is concerned with the well-being and flourishing of human life. One could even argue that, because psychology primarily concerns itself with human thought and behavior, it has a special place within the sciences (from a theological perspective) as it examines the relational and personal dimensions of humanity, which, according to Scripture, is central in Christ's work of redemption.

Providence and Common Grace

The theological vision of the created realm we have sketched so far helps form the basis for how God works in and through the human activity of psychology. Indeed, if the created realm did not have a pattern or order, then the human enterprise of science or psychology could not take place at all. But what about those who aren't already people of Christian faith? How can truths about the natural world

---

21. Megan Anna Neff and Mark R. McMinn, *Embodying Integration: A Fresh Look at Christianity in the Therapy Room* (Downers Grove, IL: IVP Academic, 2020), 163.
22. Neff and McMinn, *Embodying Integration*, 163.

be discovered from scientists or psychologists who aren't necessarily Christians or even theists? Two other theological terms help us here: providence and common grace.

After creating the world, God promises to be faithful to it and sustain it through the seasons and harvest (Gen. 8:21–23). God's care for and active sustaining of the created order serves as the basic theological understanding of providence. Although there is evil present in the world, we are reminded in Job that if God withdrew God's Spirit, then all of humanity would perish (34:14–15). God's Spirit is the Spirit of Life—the One who moves within the created world to uphold and sustain that which God has created. The Spirit also works to move persons toward salvation, and as providential provider to the created realm, God as creator speaks a continual "yes" to life that sustains creation. As theologian David Fergusson aptly puts it, "The determination of God to overcome evil and not to abandon the project of creation is a persistent theme" in Scripture.[23] God's interaction with the world is continuous and ongoing, and the doctrine of providence helps us give an account of the diversity of actions that the Spirit takes to sustain the world.

The first way that we can understand providence is in God's work to restrain evil in the world. As Christians, we believe that, although evil exists, God keeps evil at bay so that it is not as bad as it could be. At the same time, as both Christians and psychologists, we should reject notions dismissing or diminishing the reality of evil as something that is "not that bad." Evil is evil, even if those in power say that it is not. We can never dismiss the reality of pain in people's lives or invalidate the suffering that someone is currently experiencing. There is no way to easily explain here why evil does still exist, but the doctrine of providence provides an understanding that God does work to restrain evil to some degree.

A second aspect of providence that is important to point out is the way in which God allows goodness, truth, and beauty to still be present in the world, and for good things to come to all people— both for those who know God and for those who do not profess a

23. David Fergusson, *The Providence of God: A Polyphonic Approach*, Current Issues in Theology (New York: Cambridge University Press, 2019), 22.

faith in God. As Jesus reminds us, God causes the sun to rise on the evil and on the good and sends rain on both the righteous and the unrighteous (Matt. 5:45). In this verse from Matthew, we see that God's blessings still fall on those who might not acknowledge God or heed God's commands. God not only upholds the life of human and nonhuman creatures but also takes no pleasure in the death of even the wicked (Ezek. 18:23). God works toward the flourishing and well-being of creation, and although we might not recognize this activity, it speaks to the generosity and hospitality of God that is frequently present in our lives.

A third component of providence concerns how God works to allow truths about the world to be discovered by both Christians and non-Christians. This is a natural extension of the point above—namely, that God allows good things to be given to all human life—and some of this goodness is how God allows humanity to explore, discover, tend, and develop the created world that God has made. Theologians in the tradition of Abraham Kuyper have referred to these elements of God's truth being evident in the wider culture as common grace. Common grace is God's movement through the Son and Spirit to develop human culture and promote human flourishing even though sin is still present.[24] In short, God does not create a world and then step away and leave creation on its own. God graciously reaches out to creation, sustaining and perfecting the created order, allowing humanity to discover elements of creation through art, science, culture, and, yes, psychology.

In addition to the idea of common grace found in the Reformed tradition and in the writings of theologians shaped by Kuyper, we also find helpful the Wesleyan notion of prevenient grace, which overlaps with common grace to some degree. Both "common grace" and "prevenient grace" are theological terms that describe how aspects of goodness, beauty, and truth are present in the world despite the reality of sin. There is a difference among the Reformed and Wesleyan traditions concerning how (or whether) this grace leads to salvation.[25]

24. Lydia Kim-van Daalen, "The Holy Spirit, Common Grace, and Secular Psychotherapy," *Journal of Psychology and Theology* 40, no. 3 (2012): 229–39.

25. L. G. Cox, "Prevenient Grace: A Wesleyan View," *Journal of the Evangelical Theological Society* 12, no. 3 (1969): 143.

Within the Reformed tradition, common grace does not lead to salvation, whereas in the Wesleyan tradition, prevenient grace is the working in someone's life that occurs before conversion that does help lead someone to salvation. However, in the Wesleyan tradition, prevenient grace does not always lead to salvation since it can be ignored or resisted. Although they differ slightly, the important point to keep in mind here is that both theological traditions provide the necessary resources for understanding how truth can be discerned while sin is still present. Sin does disrupt the ordering of God's creation—within the human heart and in the structures and cultures of society—but it does not destroy God's good creation entirely, much less ultimately. God is committed to ensuring that sin does not have the final word regarding human and nonhuman creation, and the fullest manifestations of this commitment are the person and work of Jesus Christ and the perfecting actions of the Spirit.[26]

Kuyper's notion of discovery and development is particularly helpful for understanding the work of psychology. Certain dimensions of the created world can be *discovered* through the enterprise of science or psychology, and these discoveries can also be *developed* as a part of human culture. As Kuyper states, "The life of the world is to be honored in its independence, and . . . we must, in every domain, discover the treasures and develop the potencies hidden by God in nature and in human life."[27] For Kuyper, because humans stand in a certain relation with the world, they have the ability to discover the treasures of creation and to develop these patterns found in creation.

Providence and common grace serve as two points of theological reflection that are critical for students of psychology and Christianity, in large part because they remind us that there are truths to be learned from the study of the human creature (*discovery*), and that, as humans make meaning of these truths, they *develop* a culture around these discoveries in the form of bodies of knowledge within psychological science. God has given humans a natural curiosity

26. See Colin E. Gunton, *The Promise of Trinitarian Theology*, 2nd ed. (London: T&T Clark, 2003).

27. Abraham Kuyper, *Lectures on Calvinism* (Peabody, MA: Hendrickson, 2008), 31.

about the world around them (think about how Jean Piaget referred to children as "little scientists"), and in this curiosity we have a propensity for and are drawn toward social interaction with other humans. It also makes sense that some of this curiosity manifests itself in a basic curiosity about other humans and a desire to study these complex creatures through something like psychology (e.g., psychology is often one of the largest majors on university campuses in the United States).

Al Wolters's work *Creation Regained* offers a similar reappraisal of Kuyper but uses the terms "structure" and "direction."[28] Creation provides a *structure* (a form or certain degree of order) that enables the natural world to be studied, but it is up to the humans working in culture to give these discoveries a *direction*. For Wolters, the Christian is charged with directing their discoveries to the working of the kingdom, in whatever domain of study a person might find themselves.[29] From the perspective of a trinitarian account of creation, the Spirit is the one who makes things what they are intended to be. This can be seen in the realms of culture as humans have the potential to give further order to what is found in the created realm, and the sciences and the arts are examples of how humans further shape and give expression to what is encountered in the natural world. Understood from the perspective of providence, it is the Spirit who guides human effort in this creative and directive process. There is something good about the created world, and there is something equally good when humans use their talents and creative capacities to learn about psychology by engaging with the world that God has created.

Giving Creation a Voice

Humans have a special role within the world of discovering and developing the created realm through the psychological sciences, and this is a natural and good use of the gifts that God has given us. Creation has an order that can be discerned, but because it speaks in terms that

28. Albert M. Wolters, *Creation Regained: Biblical Basics for a Reformational Worldview* (Grand Rapids: Eerdmans, 2005), 10.

29. Wolters, *Creation Regained*, 11–12.

are often vague and ambiguous, it is left up to humans as agents or stewards of creation to articulate the wonders of the created order through their various endeavors. Whether plowing a farm, painting a work of art, performing research on human behavior, or exploring human nature and behavior through clinical work, humans are shaping the world. We are not the first to suggest that truth can be discovered through psychology, but there has been limited discussion regarding how psychology as a discovery-oriented enterprise contributes to God's mandate of not only developing or fashioning the earth but also giving creation a voice.[30]

This approach to creation suggests that truth may be discovered and human life informed and nourished from sources that are not explicitly theological, such as psychology. For example, psychology provides us with a means for articulating the various forms and structures of human thought, feelings, and behavior found in creation. In fact, it becomes increasingly difficult to understand how psychology might contribute to our knowledge and understanding of the world if we operate with a theology that does not affirm that part of our stewardship role is to develop the created realm through psychological discoveries. At its most basic, psychology is the exploration of the human person and behavior, but it can also be understood theologically as fulfilling our task as human creatures in exploring, developing, and shaping creation in a particular way. God has created humans with the ability to explore, wonder, dream about, and develop creation, and psychology provides us with a unique opportunity for doing so. Because God has ordered the world in such a way that it is knowable to the one who investigates and explores, the created realm presents a reality that has an intrinsic logic. Thus, psychological scientists are right to assume that there are forms or patterns in the natural order that can be investigated and that psychological research not only helps discover truths about the created realm but also helps develop these truths.

All told, interactions with the material world are a necessary part of being human. Our physical world shapes and orients the cognitive,

30. Jeremy Begbie, *Voicing Creation's Praise: Towards a Theology of the Arts* (Edinburgh: T&T Clark, 1991).

social, and emotional dimensions of personhood, which means that what happens to and within the created world ultimately has significance for the ways that we become persons.[31] Because the world is unified and ordered in a certain way, humans have been given the ability to investigate and explore the patterns found in creation and ultimately to give articulation to the order and patterns that are found regarding human thought and behavior. At the same time, human personhood is also shaped by the world that we inhabit through discoveries and development. What is more, these discoveries hold the potential for being developed and directed in certain ways, and for the Christian, these developments are offered up for the ultimate glory of God's kingdom. While not all theories in psychology entirely align with the Christian gospel, one can still conceive of psychology as part of the human exploration of the created order that God has established.

Questions for Reflection and Discussion

1. What have you discovered in your own psychological studies that has allowed you to know more about God's creation (human or nonhuman)?

2. What are some of the ways you might be able to direct creation in and through your studies and work as a psychologist?

3. What are the benefits of seeing the contributions of non-Christians in terms of common grace? What might the drawbacks be?

4. Much of the discussion has focused on general revelation and common grace. How might the Christian concept of special revelation expand or develop what we find in and through the psychological sciences?

---

31. For a compelling take on how our physical environs constitute us as the physical creatures we are, see Warren S. Brown and Brad D. Strawn, *The Physical Nature of Christian Life: Neuroscience, Psychology, and the Church* (New York: Cambridge University Press, 2012).

Resources for Reading and Exploration

Fergusson, David. *Creation*. Guides to Theology. Grand Rapids: Eerdmans, 2014.

LaCugna, Catherine Mowry. *God for Us: The Trinity and Christian Life*. San Francisco: HarperSanFrancisco, 1991.

Moltmann, Jürgen. *God in Creation: A New Theology of Creation and the Spirit of God*. Minneapolis: Fortress, 1993.

3

God's Wider Presence

Key takeaways from this chapter:

- Psychological practitioners are helped by a broader notion of God's presence in the world.
- The Spirit of God is present and active outside the church and without reference to Jesus Christ.
- The Spirit is not a disembodied ghost but the divine breath of life.
- God is actively involved in our colleagues' and clients' lives long before and long after our own involvement.

Meet John. He's eighteen years old. He can be sarcastic, temperamental, and disengaged at times, but, just as often, he's inquisitive, kind, and self-reflective. He plans on going to college at some point in the future, but he really isn't interested in taking on the kind of student debt he's heard so much about. In the meantime, he's pretty content working at a local coffee shop and playing bass with the band he formed with his friends from high school.

Like many in his generational cohort, John also lives with a base level of anxiety that manifests itself in semi-frequent bouts of depression. It's not that he hates his life or can't recognize how, as a middle-class White kid from the suburbs, his problems are qualitatively different than most of the humans on the planet. If anything, that's part of the problem. On the surface, it doesn't appear that he would have much to fret about, and he knows it, but he can't seem to shake the pervasive sense of dread that serves as the backdrop for his every waking moment.

Because it's Tuesday, John is your first client of the day. Scanning through your files in preparation for your time together, you are reminded that, like an increasing number of his contemporaries, John is a religious "none." He doesn't identify with any religious tradition and never really has. He was raised in a nonreligious home, and while he isn't antagonistic toward any specific religion or people of faith in general, religion has no bearing on his daily life—at least not in any significant way. If pressed, John would probably say that he just doesn't see what the fuss is all about. Religious beliefs and practices are less than irrelevant to him. They are simply beside the point.

John is not an outlier. In fact, as you sit knee-to-knee with him on this Tuesday morning, you realize that most of your clients, whether they profess some kind of religious faith or not, share a profile similar to John. Unlike John, they may identify as Christian and even engage in some of the more formal practices that being a Christian often entails (e.g., church attendance, financial giving, and observance of certain holidays). But for all intents and purposes, this identity has no real purchase on the way they live, much less how they understand their lives. Even those whose Christian faith is central to their identity come to you first and foremost for psychotherapy and not pastoral counseling, so they have no real expectation that religion would or should come into play.

Recognizing that this kind of religious diversity is part of what makes US society so rich and textured, the American Psychological Association code of ethics has made it clear that, regardless of a client's religious commitments (or lack thereof), psychologists are to be "aware of and respect cultural, individual and role differences, including those based on . . . religion . . . and consider these factors when working with members of such groups." At the same time, "In their work-related activities, psychologists do not engage in unfair discrimination based on . . . religion . . . or any basis proscribed by law."[1] In other words, although psychologists must be sensitive to the various ways in which religion and spirituality might be functioning in a client's life, it would never be appropriate for therapists to impose their beliefs and values on clients, or to provide differential treatment to individuals who may not subscribe to those same beliefs and values.

In some respects, formal codes of conduct like these make things fairly straightforward. It can often be helpful for therapists to know exactly what to do when attempting to navigate real-world complexities. If a client wants to talk about their religion or spirituality, great. If not, no problem. In fact, even though it's perfectly understandable for clients to turn to their therapist for guidance on matters of faith, they are likely to be disappointed when they do. After all, clinical psychologists are trained in forms of psychotherapy and not in theology. Only in rare cases are they also members of the clergy.[2]

Complicating matters, however, is the way in which formal codes of conduct, although at times helpful, can mask (and perhaps even sublimate) much deeper issues. As Kenneth Pargament has pointed out, contemporary models of psychotherapy have inherited a deep suspicion regarding religion and spirituality from the psychological paradigms that emerged during the twentieth century, most notably behaviorism and psychoanalysis.[3] According to Pargament, this disciplinary skepticism—and, at times, outright hostility—has generated thin and superficial notions of religious faith among many (if not most) psychotherapists in practice today. What is more, because the great majority of psychology programs in the United States provide virtually no training in religion or spirituality, graduates of these programs are largely unprepared to help, much less understand, clients

1. American Psychological Association, "Ethical Principles of Psychologists and Code of Conduct," 2017, https://www.apa.org/ethics/code.
2. Our colleagues at Fuller Seminary, Dr. Siang-Yang Tan, Dr. Brad Strawn, and Dr. Pamela Ebstyne-King, are notable exceptions to this rule.
3. Kenneth I. Pargament, *Spiritually Integrated Psychotherapy: Understanding and Addressing the Sacred* (New York: Guilford Press, 2007), 8.

whose religious life and practice are central to their identity.[4] Never-theless, regardless of the gaps in their training or their personal con-victions, APA guidelines stipulate that therapists must address their clients' religious and spiritual concerns in the midst of psychotherapy when appropriate.[5] It is in part for this very reason that psychologists like David A. Steere have advocated strongly for all mental health workers—from psychotherapists, psychologists, and psychiatrists, to social workers, pastoral counselors, and nurses—to accommodate a spiritual dimension in their work.[6]

To be sure, these are significant challenges for anyone studying to become a clinical psychologist, but students of Christian faith face an even larger and more pressing question from the start—one that is distinctly theological. Namely, in what sense does their work as mental health professionals relate to the ongoing presence and activity of God in the world? Do their current studies or their future roles in the field of psychology have anything to do with the ways in which God is involved in their own lives, or are these wholly separate proj-ects that, for necessary reasons, need to be kept free from all things theological? As it concerns a client like John, in what ways (if any) might God be involved in *his* journey toward healing and mental health? For that matter, what does it look like for any of us to par-ticipate faithfully in what God is doing in our clients' lives, even in those cases when the topics of faith, spirituality, and/or religion are, for good reason, never broached?

In our estimation, the only way to answer these questions without throwing our hands up and concluding that the realms of psychology

4. Pargament cites two key studies suggesting that "only 18% of the directors [of counseling psychology programs in the United States] indicated that their graduate programs offered a course that focused on religion or spirituality (Schulte, Skinner, & Claiborn, 2002). Only 13% of training directors of clinical psychology programs in the United States and Canada reported that their curriculum included a course on religion and spirituality (Brawer, Handal, Fabricatore, Roberts, & Wajda-Johnston, 2002)." *Spiritually Integrated Psychotherapy*, 9.

5. An odd sort of disciplinary ambivalence has emerged. As Steven J. Sandage and Jeannine K. Brown point out, "During the past forty years, the fields of psychology and psychotherapy have experienced a profound shift on the topics of 'religion' and 'spirituality,' even as the formal disciplines of theology and religious studies remain largely marginalized within psychology." *Relational Integration*, 30.

6. See David A. Steere, *Spiritual Presence in Psychotherapy: A Guide for Caregivers* (New York: Routledge, 2018).

and theology should remain wholly distinct is to develop a much broader and more generous notion of God's presence.[7] In fact, a more robust pneumatology (i.e., a doctrine of the Spirit) is critical for recognizing and affirming the ways in which humans are able to collaborate with God's activity in the broader world, especially in domains (e.g., the therapeutic context) that are not explicitly Christian, religious, or even theistic. While the doctrine of creation provides a foundation for conceptualizing the relationship between psychology and the Christian faith, pneumatology is the doctrine that can help students of psychology recognize how God's action is carried out through human involvement in clinical and research psychology.

In this chapter, then, we develop a biblically grounded pneumatology that conceives of the Spirit primarily in terms of the presence and ongoing activity of God's Spirit in the world, and not merely as the Spirit of Christ and his church. In doing so, we will ask two basic questions: What is God up to? and How do we join in?[8]

A God without Borders

In the previous chapter, we briefly considered a handful of distinct but overlapping theological concepts: general revelation, common

7. We are by no means the first to make this claim about the Spirit's presence in the midst of therapy. See, for example, the excellent work of Siang-Yang Tan in *Counseling and Psychotherapy: A Christian Perspective* (Grand Rapids: Baker Academic, 2011); and Siang-Yang Tan and Douglas H. Gregg, *Disciplines of the Holy Spirit: How to Connect to the Spirit's Power and Presence* (Grand Rapids: Zondervan, 1997). Our goal here is not to introduce an entirely novel concept that is without precedent, but rather to develop a constructive theology of the Spirit that might fill some gaps in the current literature and offer a more robust series of theological and biblical resources for psychologists (and psychologists in training) hoping to answer the question of how their work as clinicians relates to God's larger project in the world.

8. Even though this book is concerned primarily with developing a more robust way of doing constructive theology and not so much with "integration" per se, the question of how the therapist participates with God's ongoing mission in the world through the work of clinical psychology reflects the leading edge of the current integration conversation. See, for example, Megan Anna Neff and Mark R. McMinn, *Embodying Integration: A Fresh Look at Christianity in the Therapy Room* (Downers Grove, IL: IVP Academic, 2020). Indeed, Neff and McMinn conclude their text by raising the same question we are exploring: What is God up to in the world?

grace, and natural theology. These are related topics, to be sure, and they each provide a slightly different way of thinking not only about how God discloses Godself in and through the natural realm but also about how God structures, orders, and actively upholds the whole of the created order. Indeed, one of our operating assumptions is that the self-disclosure of the trinitarian God in creation is not simply an interesting aside to the "real" truth we find in Scripture but rather serves as the necessary condition for humans to discover anything at all about God's wisdom, beauty, and creativity in their exploration of the world we inhabit. Without any risk of overstatement, none of the claims we are advancing in this book regarding the theological significance of the psychological sciences hold up without a well-rounded conception of the trinitarian God revealing Godself in and through the created order.

However, we also noted that, depending on the historical and denominational context in which it was discussed, each concept has proven to be somewhat problematic. For example, motivated by their commitment to *sola Scriptura*, theologians in the Reformed tradition have explored at great length the numerous occasions in which the biblical witness points toward God's revelatory work in the world.[9] Yet, more often than not, these theologians have tended to understand this mode of God's revelation as a "cup half empty."[10] When compared to the special revelation found in Scripture and the person and work of Jesus Christ, the knowledge of God that is disclosed through general revelation is thought to be at best ambiguous, vague, and inchoate, and at worst, prone to distortion and abuse by a sin-scarred humanity.[11] For many, the distorting effects of human sin are

9. Calvin's work on the topic was expansive and robust. As a consequence, many of the Reformed theologians writing in the shadow of Calvin have been in an ongoing argument regarding who is most faithful, not so much to the biblical text but to Calvin.

10. We owe this turn of phrase to Robert K. Johnston, "The Mystery Discerning Business," in *Don't Stop Believin': Pop Culture and Religion from Ben Hur to Zombies*, ed. Robert K. Johnston, Craig Detweiler, and Barry Taylor (Louisville: Westminster John Knox Press, 2012), 211–12.

11. This captures much of the core argument outlined by G. C. Berkouwer, *General Revelation* (Grand Rapids: Eerdmans, 1955); and Bruce A. Demarest, *General Revelation: Historical Views and Contemporary Issues* (Grand Rapids: Zondervan, 1982).

simply too great a hurdle to overcome, which means that the primary function of general revelation is to prepare people to receive the more complete, saving knowledge of God in Christ. From this perspective, general revelation can do little more than reveal to humans that they are without excuse for denying that which creation has routinely made clear to them (Rom. 1:20) and thus stand condemned before a righteous God.

In addition to this pervasive skepticism regarding the human capacity to deduce any kind of reliable or trustworthy knowledge about God from the created order, some theologians have also raised legitimate concerns about whether the doctrine of general revelation involves God at all. The reason Karl Barth said "*Nein!*" so forcefully to the natural theology espoused by his fellow German theologians was not because he had a limited vision of how God worked in the world but because he was wary of any theological project that would suggest humans could, through unaided reason or by simply observing the natural order, arrive at any kind of knowledge of God.[12] For it to be revelation, said Barth, something more than mere human curiosity needs to be in play. Only God can reveal Godself. To suggest otherwise runs the risk of humans "discovering" a God who looks an awful lot like a projection of themselves.[13]

Although we don't share all the concerns our theological forebears articulated, we highlight them in order to situate our understanding of God's wider presence[14] within the historic theological tradition.

12. See Emil Brunner and Karl Barth, *Natural Theology: Comprising "Nature and Grace"* (London: Centenary Press, 1946).

13. Even though Barth overstated his case, he was right. The German church's acquiescence to Hitler's rise to power was, in no small part, due to a natural theology that had no need for God's active agency in the human pursuit of knowledge about God. In this respect, Ludwig Feuerbach's famous critique in *The Essence of Christianity* was shown to be true: "God" is just "human" shouted loudly.

14. We would like to acknowledge our indebtedness for this phrasing to Robert K. Johnston, *God's Wider Presence: Reconsidering General Revelation* (Grand Rapids: Baker Academic, 2014). Because Johnston's book interacts with, draws from, and, indeed, builds on our previous work on this topic, it is encouraging to see that the theological discourse in which we have played a small part is now serving as the theological and biblical touchstone for those exploring the question of how the practice of clinical psychology relates to the presence and activity of God in the world. A recent example of psychologists who explicitly cite Johnston's notion of God's wider presence as their theological starting point are Steven J. Sandage and Jeannine K. Brown,

For example, we agree with the Reformed theologians that sin clouds our vision and that its distorting effects should not be taken lightly. But just because we see "through a glass darkly" does not mean that we should automatically distrust, discount, or devalue the truths we discover in and through our encounter with the world. If this were the case, then neither should we trust the truths we encounter in Scripture, for they too are filtered through our sin-marred faculties. In our present state, sin is of course a given, but to borrow a phrase from Emil Brunner, there remains a "point of contact" between God and humanity.[15]

This point of contact is more than a mere interface by which theological knowledge is transmitted. Rather, it implies the coming together of two subjects or, in the words of Martin Buber, an "I-Thou" encounter.[16] To speak of God's wider presence in this way is to shift the frame of reference from what humans know *about* God to the means by which humans come to *know* God personally. It is to acknowledge that, as the Third Person of the Trinity, the Spirit of God is always already present and active in human life, meeting people in the midst of concrete, lived situations. Just as Barth suggested, there simply is no sense in which humans, through their own efforts, could ever attain a knowledge of God without God's ongoing involvement in their various pursuits. But in contrast to Barth, our operating assumption is that the Spirit of God is pervasively present in the world rather than standing at an "infinite qualitative distance" from humanity, which means that God is not simply waiting around passively for humans to discover some generic set of divine attributes through unaided human reason.[17] The Spirit of God is actively calling

---

Relational Integration of Psychology and Christian Theology: Theory, Research, and Practice (New York: Routledge, 2018), 94–95.

15. The bulk of the conversation between Barth and Brunner focuses on the possibility (or lack thereof) of this "point of contact." See Barth and Brunner, *Natural Theology*.

16. Martin Buber, *I and Thou*, trans. Ronald Gregor Smith (Mansfield Centre, CT: Martino, 2010).

17. In his commentary on Romans, Barth was particularly influenced by Søren Kierkegaard's notion of an "infinite qualitative" difference or distinction between God and humanity. See Søren Kierkegaard, *Training in Christianity and the Edifying Discourse Which "Accompanied" It*, trans. Walter Lowrie (Oxford: Oxford University Press, 1941), 139.

human creatures to participate as co-laborers in God's creative project, inviting them to "search for God and perhaps grope around for him and find him" (Acts 17:27).

These key differences notwithstanding, we remain fully in line with the broader Protestant tradition in our commitment to a biblically grounded understanding of the Spirit's wider presence. Indeed, this commitment to grappling with the biblical text and its testimony to God's common grace is perhaps one of the Reformed tradition's greatest contributions to contemporary constructive theology. For, more so than any other source, it is the biblical witness that not only calls into question any overly narrow or restrictive view of God's work in the world but also challenges us to take seriously the variety of ways in which God is very much present and active outside the church and without reference to Jesus Christ.

Although space will not permit an exhaustive account of the biblical data, we can identify at least three domains in which God reveals Godself in Scripture, each of which has been outlined by Robert K. Johnston in *God's Wider Presence*:

> It is my contention that God's wider revelation is not something that is available to all humanity through the *imago Dei* based on our human capacity. Rather, with [Karl] Barth, we must say, first, that revelation always needs the Spirit as Revealer—it is event. Secondly, with [Friedrich] Schleiermacher, general revelation is not first of all accessible because of our rationality, but rather is rooted in that intuition of Something or Someone beyond us and our feeling that results from this encounter. And third, with [C. S.] Lewis . . . general revelation is not merely a trace, something largely insignificant given Christ or incomprehensible because of our sin, but the experience of the wider Presence of God through his Spirit mediated through *creation, conscience*, and *human culture*.[18]

Creation, conscience, and human culture: let us turn briefly to each of these modes by which the Spirit is present in our lives before considering what it might look like to participate with the Spirit in and through the work of clinical psychology.

18. Johnston, *God's Wider Presence*, 127–28 (emphasis added).

Creation

From the book of Job (32:8) to various psalms (8:3–4; 19:1–6; 93:3; 97:6) to the stories found in the Acts of the Apostles (14:15–17; 17:24–28) to the opening chapters of Romans (1:18–20), Scripture is filled with references to God's revelatory presence mediated through nature and the created order more generally. When the "heavens declare the glory of God" (Ps. 19:1 NIV), or when the psalmist looks to the heavens and sees "the work of [God's] fingers" (Ps. 8:3 NIV), no caveat is provided. There is no suggestion by the biblical authors nor is there anything about the narrative context of these passages that would indicate the knowledge creation provides regarding God's creative work is incomplete or inadequate. Its function is not merely to "prepare" humans to receive a more complete form of revelation; rather, the Spirit's pervasive presence in nature is simply a given. Thus, the divine *ruach* (i.e., spirit) hovering over the watery abyss during creation (Gen. 1:2) is the same Spirit who actively sustains and upholds God's ongoing creative project. Nothing is more fundamental. For the biblical authors, the Spirit of God constitutes material reality itself.

Conscience

In addition to the heavens and earth proclaiming the work of God, the biblical text also indicates that God is actively present in the human heart, even among those who are neither part of the covenant community nor privy to the special revelation found in the person of Christ. For instance, according to the apostle Paul, "When Gentiles, who do not possess the law, do instinctively what the law requires, these, though not having the law, are a law to themselves. They show that what the law requires is written on their hearts, to which their own conscience also bears witness; and their conflicting thoughts will accuse or perhaps excuse them on the day when, according to my gospel, God, through Jesus Christ, will judge the secret thoughts of all" (Rom. 2:14–16 NRSV).

There is far too much in these few verses to fully unpack here. What we can say is that Paul's larger argument in Romans underscores the fact that all have sinned—everyone. No one, whether Jew or gentile, is worthy of God's unmerited grace. But within that argument, in which we are all sinners, Paul is both honest and humble enough to say that some of us who know God and fail to do God's will are put to shame by those who don't have God's special revelation. They may not have any knowledge of Jesus or the law, but they nonetheless act consistent with God's revelation. What the law requires is "written on their hearts," and their conscience bears witness to this reality. Paul's point is not that we don't need Jesus or that special revelation is not essential. His point is rather that people outside the covenant community of Israel and outside the Christian faith can and do know God's will and, more important, they do it. To borrow a turn of phrase from biblical scholar Robert Jewett, these "righteous Gentiles" are able to sense and discern what God has written on their hearts and to respond appropriately.[19] Another way to put it is that they are respond-able to the presence and activity of the Spirit of God. And according to Paul, somehow, and in some way, they will be accused or excused based on how they respond when the Spirit pricks their conscience.

Culture

One of the distinguishing marks of what it means to be human is that we are culture-makers through and through. As evolutionary psychologists frequently remind us, it's almost as if we cannot help but make something of the world we inhabit. Humans construct the very niches that, in turn, form and inform our development as individuals and as a species.[20] Theologically speaking, this stands to reason. Not only do humans "image" the Creator through their creative projects, but their culture-making activity serves as one of the primary means by which they are able to collaborate with God's creative project. In an important sense, God created humans to be

19. Robert Jewett, *Saint Paul at the Movies: The Apostle's Dialogue with American Culture* (Louisville: Westminster John Knox, 1993), 65–76.
20. Two recent examples of evolutionary psychologists making claims along these lines are Michael Tomasello, *Becoming Human: A Theory of Ontogeny* (Cambridge, MA: Belknap Press, 2019); and Robert Boyd, *A Different Kind of Animal: How Culture Transformed Our Species* (Princeton: Princeton University Press, 2018).

not simply managers of creation but cocreators, ascribing to them the task of being "fruitful," multiplying, and filling the created order (Gen. 1:28). Known as the cultural mandate, humans are to "till" the soil and "keep" it, that is, to cultivate it (Gen. 2:15 NRSV). As visual artist Makoto Fujimura says so eloquently in his book *Culture Care*, "Culture is not a territory to be won or lost but a resource we are called to steward with care. Culture is a garden to be cultivated."[21]

When located within a larger theological framework of God's revelatory presence, human culture-making serves as an occasion in which God is not only present but actively collaborates with humans. In Exodus, it is the Spirit of God who fills the artisans and craftsmen responsible for both the construction and adornment of the tabernacle (Exod. 31:1–11; 36:8–13). But it is not merely artists in the covenant community who are in-spirited in this way. As Paul points out in his speech on the Areopagus, the same Spirit who filled the artisans building the tabernacle is the One who also inspired the Greek poets to create art that reflected the truth of God's pervasive presence: "In him we live and move and have our being" (Acts 17:28 NRSV). Rather than focus on how this poetry could only ever deliver "partial" knowledge about God or how the Athenians' minds were distorted by sin, Paul points out the ways in which the Spirit of God is already present and active in their creative works, even when those works of art were produced in a cultural context that knew nothing of the person and work of Jesus Christ or the God of Israel.

Not all biblical scholars agree that Paul was uncritically endorsing this Greek poetry. Nevertheless, there is no escaping the fact that now we have a series of cultural artifacts (i.e., poems), produced by non-Christian authors, included in the Christian canon as a testament to God's reality-encompassing presence (e.g., Acts 17:18). More to the point, though, by adopting this kind of posture toward a pre-Christian culture, Paul's approach serves as a helpful model for anyone hoping to participate in what the Spirit is up to in contemporary, post-Christian societies.

21. Makoto Fujimura, *Culture Care: Reconnecting with Beauty for Our Common Life* (Downers Grove, IL: IVP Books, 2017), 22.

The Breath of God

We have only scratched the surface of the biblical evidence here, but there is plenty to reinforce the claim that the Spirit of God is indeed present and active far beyond the walls of the church and in places where the name of Jesus is never uttered. Still, even if we accept this basic premise as the starting point for a more robust pneumatology, the question remains as to what it would look like to contribute to or participate in the Spirit's ongoing project in the world. It is a question that of course pertains to every person of faith, no matter what their individual vocation happens to be. As the cultural mandate of Genesis suggests, we have all been entrusted with the task of co-laboring with God, called to cultivate our particular corner of the garden in such a way that it bears life. However, given that clinical psychologists and psychological scientists often operate in domains that, for legal and ethical reasons, are devoid of any explicitly Christian references, the question of how this kind of work contributes to the Spirit's work is particularly critical for students of psychology to consider.

For anyone whose imagination has been shaped by the Western intellectual tradition, the idea that humans might interact with any "spirit," much less the Spirit of God, may present certain difficulties, but this need not be the case. In contrast to the Latin *spiritus* or the German *geist*, the biblical text has no conception of the human or divine spirit as disembodied ghosts or immaterial beings. Rather, the authors of the Hebrew Bible conceive of the Spirit of God as the divine *ruach*, which is best translated not as spirit but as wind, breath, or sustaining energy. *Ruach* is the breath of life that perpetually animates the whole of the created order (Eccles. 3:21; 11:5; 12:7), the irresistible force of the Creator's power, which ushers in both God's wrath and God's life-giving presence (Ezek. 13:13; 36:26–27).

According to Jürgen Moltmann, who developed one of the most influential pneumatologies of the twentieth century, *ruach* is at once "God's own creative power to give life, and the created ability to live enjoyed by all the living (Ps. 104:30)."[22] For Moltmann, the Spirit's creative work is not cut off from our embodied life in the natural

---

22. Jürgen Moltmann, *The Spirit of Life: A Universal Affirmation*, trans. Margaret Kohl (Minneapolis: Fortress, 1992), 41.

world; rather, God's *ruach* serves as "the divine wellspring of life—the source of life created, life preserved and life daily renewed, and finally the source of the eternal life of all created being."[23] From a biblical perspective, then, there is a necessary blurring of the boundaries between the activities of God's Spirit and the human spirit. God's *ruach* not only brings the first humans to life by breathing into the dust (Gen. 2:7), it also "returns" to God when the lives of those creatures come to an end (Eccles. 12:7). According to the biblical testimony, it isn't that humans simply live their lives under their own power until the appointed time at which God determines they should no longer exist; it is rather that their every waking moment is animated and upheld by the Spirit of God who is actively breathing life into the world. In fact, as Psalm 104:29 (and even Ehud in Job 34:15) makes clear, if the Spirit were not present, there would be nothing and no one of which we could even speak, so much so that it would be more accurate to consider humans as in-spirited bodies.[24]

Importantly, though, while the biblical authors do indeed use the word *ruach* to talk about both the divine Spirit and the human spirit, they do not fully equate the human and divine spirit, nor do they completely collapse the distinction between the two. We too can picture our own spirits as a wind or a breath, like God's *ruach*, but it is a breath of a different sort. So, on the one hand, the biblical witness speaks of *ruach* as the Spirit of God in the world, but, on the other hand, in speaking of humans and human creations, it often employs the image of *hevel*. This is the word that the preacher in Ecclesiastes repeats time and again, and it is often translated as "meaningless" or "vanity." But in that book and elsewhere, *hevel* is better translated as vapor, steam, or breath. Consider Psalm 39: "Surely everyone stands as a mere breath [*hevel*]. Surely everyone goes about like a shadow. Surely for nothing they are in turmoil [*hevel*]; they heap up, and do not know who will gather. . . . Surely everyone is a mere breath [*hevel*]" (vv. 5–6, 11 NRSV). In other words, the human is as fleeting

---

23. Moltmann, *The Spirit of Life*, 82.

24. We don't have the space to unpack this philosophically and theologically loaded claim. For those who are interested in the implications of such a view, we point readers to Nancey Murphy's excellent *Bodies and Souls, or Spirited Bodies? Current Issues in Theology* (Cambridge, MA: Cambridge University Press, 2006).

and insubstantial as the condensation we see when we exhale a warm breath into the cold night air. Like the clearing of a fog or mist, as soon as it's here, it's gone.[25]

Of course, as long as there is no movement in the air (e.g., in a vacuum), a mist or vapor of this sort will remain suspended indefinitely. It is only under the force of a stronger wind—a stronger breath—that the mist seemingly disappears. In fact, though, the condensed water particles hovering together in the air are not destroyed or annihilated. Rather, they yield themselves; they give way to another breath. They are at once caught up in and dissipated by the wind. The vapor is still present, but in its disruption, it is re-created and reconstituted.[26]

This image of a fleeting vapor under the influence of the moving wind is particularly fitting for students of psychology considering how their research and clinical work might relate to the movement of God's Spirit, especially because many of their efforts with clients will likely never see the light of day and, even if they do, will seem fleeting at best. They are but a breath. As a consequence, the image of an ephemeral mist (*hevel*) interacting with a gale-force current (*ruach*) serves as a helpful metaphor for considering what it looks like to participate in God's ongoing project in the world. In doing so, it offers us a picture of what takes place any time the divine Spirit meets and merges with the human spirit.

The Spirit Animates

In the first place, as the breath of life, the Spirit of God serves as the animating force behind each and every one of our initiatives,

25. We have covered elsewhere much of what we are outlining here regarding the Hebrew concepts of *hevel* and *ruach*. See, e.g., Kutter Callaway, *Scoring Transcendence: Contemporary Film Music as Religious Experience* (Waco: Baylor University Press, 2013), 162–71. That being said, we were pleasantly surprised to discover that Megan Anna Neff and Mark R. McMinn also find the image of *hevel* helpful for thinking about our contemporary world. For anyone interested in a more developed account of how the book of Ecclesiastes can serve as a much-needed conversation partner for those engaged in clinical psychology, we highly recommend their book, *Embodying Integration: A Fresh Look at Christianity in the Therapy Room* (Downers Grove, IL: IVP Academic, 2020).

26. We owe this particular way of thinking about the interaction between *hevel* and *ruach* to Jean-Luc Marion, *God without Being*, 2nd ed., trans. Thomas A. Carlson (Chicago: University of Chicago Press, 2012).

from the remarkable to the mundane. Theologically speaking, no human activity takes place outside the Spirit's purview, and that includes the work of mental health professionals. Even if we wanted to section off some domain of life (e.g., clinical psychology) from the Spirit's influence, it would not be possible, for the *ruach Elohim* is a pervasive presence that animates the whole of our life in the world. Just as Psalm 139:7 rightly asks, "Where can I go from your spirit? Or where can I flee from your presence?" (NRSV). Here the psalmist is asking a far deeper question than whether an actual location might exist in which the Spirit is not already present. Rather, as the all-pervasive, animating force of life, the Spirit is actively present in our every proceeding as the internal structure that makes any and every human interaction possible.[27]

To use a term coined by John V. Taylor, as the animating force of life, the Spirit is the "go-between God," the One who creates the necessary conditions not only for us to be aware of the "other" in our midst but also for us to recognize the full potential of those sacred moments in which we encounter another person for who they truly are.[28] From this perspective, to ask how our various human projects (psychological or otherwise) would unfold in the Spirit's absence is as nonsensical as asking what a group of fictional literary characters might do in the absence of their author. The author doesn't merely intervene in the lives of these characters, occasionally influencing their otherwise self-sustaining activities; rather, the author constitutes the conditions for their very existence. Without the author's ongoing, creative involvement, there simply are no characters and there is no story. It is in this strong sense that the Spirit animates our lives and the world we inhabit.

The Spirit Disrupts

The idea of a vapor or mist giving way to a stronger wind might strike some as a fairly innocuous metaphor, but if we think of it in

---

27. The theological term most often used to describe this internal structuring by the Spirit is "immanent transcendence."

28. John Vernon Taylor, *The Go-Between God: The Holy Spirit and the Christian Mission* (London: SCM, 2004).

terms of God's Spirit engaging with the human spirit, a far more disruptive and unsettling picture emerges. For instance, it is not incidental that the most disruptive voices in Israel's history were the prophets and judges who, stirred by the Spirit of God, announced God's judgment on a hard-hearted and wayward people (Judg. 3:10; 6:34; 11:29; 13:25; Ezek. 11:5; Mic. 3:8; Zech. 7:12). If there is one thing the Spirit refuses to leave untouched, it's the status quo. In fact, disrupting our staid sensibilities is so central to the Spirit's ongoing work that, according to Walter Brueggemann, the primary role of the spirit-filled prophet is to invite disruption into our midst:

> The poetic practice of Jeremiah is an invitation to seek for language that is passionate, dangerous, and imaginative enough to make available the passion, danger and freedom of God who summons us to God's own conflict. It is always a practice of such prophetic poetry to break the conventions in which we habituate God. The dulled God of the conventional religious traditions will never yield energy for ministry. But this poetry gives us hints and permissions about bringing this conflict-making God to speech. Otherwise, we may miss the conflict which is our poetic, prophetic vocation.[29]

If Jeremiah's prophetic ministry is any indication, to participate in the Spirit's work is not to rest comfortably in a stable and predictable environment. It is rather to open oneself up to a radical form of disruption, inviting the Spirit to break the conventions in which we habituate the divine, and, in doing so, to bring this conflict-making God to speech.

The Spirit Decenters

The Spirit's disruptive work is particularly unsettling for those who are located at or near centers of power. A case in point is King Josiah's stand against a foreign adversary. One of Judah's good kings (2 Chron. 34:2), Josiah is best known for the various reforms he instituted during his reign. Second Chronicles 35:20–27 tells the story of Josiah's death, which begins when Neco, the king of Egypt, attempts

---

29. Walter Breuggemann, *Hopeful Imagination: Prophetic Voices in Exile* (Philadelphia: Fortress, 1986), 15.

to cross through Israel on his way to battle another nation. Rather than allowing the Egyptian army to pass through peacefully, Josiah intercepts Neco, which prompts the Egyptian pharaoh to ask, "What have I to do with you, king of Judah? I am not coming against you today, but against the house with which I am at war; and God has commanded me to hurry. Cease opposing God, who is with me, so that he will not destroy you" (2 Chron. 35:21 NRSV). According to the text, Josiah refuses to "listen to the words of Neco from the mouth of God" (2 Chron. 35:22 NRSV) and, as a consequence, dies from the wounds he incurs in battle, just as Neco said he would.

Again, this story is nothing if not disturbing, especially for those who identify as members of the community of faith. But that's just as it should be. After all, if anyone has the right to speak for God, surely it's the good and faithful king ruling over Yahweh's covenant community and not the king of a brutal and marauding nation like Egypt. Yet, as Josiah's story suggests, even the chosen people of God are not always (or perhaps ever?) the center around which the Spirit's operations revolve. As it turns out, Josiah's failure to realize that the initiatives of the faithful do not stand at the center of God's activity in the world was not simply a misstep; it was, in a very real sense, to actively oppose God (v. 21). In this way, Josiah's story is not unique. To borrow again from Taylor, the Spirit repeatedly "goes to great lengths to teach a particular tribe that it is God's chosen people, only to reveal to them that other nations have known the same salvation-history: 'Are you Israelites not like Cushites to me? Says the Lord. Did I not bring Israel up from Egypt, the Philistines from Caphtor, the Arameans from Kir?' (Amos 9:7)."[30]

Biblical stories like these suggest that the Spirit's decentering work operates on at least two levels. On the corporate level, the Spirit upends the unjust power structures of religious communities, nation-states, and the powerful elite who lead them. But, just as Josiah discovered, the Spirit also decenters each of us on an individual level, reconfiguring our personal sense of self. Needless to say, interacting with the Spirit in this way can be painful. In Josiah's case, it was fatal, in large part because, just like us, Josiah lived as if his personal

---

30. Taylor, *Go-Between God*, 179.

identity (as the king of God's chosen people) was a possession as well as a position, something that had to be pried from his hands. Moving in quite the opposite direction, the Spirit perpetually calls, invites, and even persuades us to locate the center of our personal identity not "within" ourselves but "outside" ourselves—to receive it as a gift from God.

Clinical psychologist Richard Beck refers to this kind of decentered sense of self as an "eccentric identity," which he argues was the defining characteristic of Jesus's life. Following the work of Arthur McGill, Beck suggests that Jesus's identity was the product of his complete and utter reliance on the decentering Spirit of God.

> The center of Jesus' reality is not within Jesus himself. Everything that happens to him, everything that is done by him, including his death, is displaced to another context and is thereby reinterpreted. However, this portrayal is understood to be a true reflection of Jesus' own way of existing. He himself does not live out of himself. He lives, so to speak, from beyond himself. Jesus does not confront his followers as a center which reveals himself. He confronts them as always revealing what is beyond him.[31]

For Beck, then, the key to Jesus's identity is that he didn't actually possess it; instead, he received it as a gift. Animated at every turn by the Spirit, Jesus lived a fully decentered life. And we are invited to do the same. On both the corporate and personal level, we participate with the Spirit's decentering work any time we too embrace an eccentric identity—a deep sense of self that is anchored not merely outside of ourselves, but ultimately, in God.

The Spirit Disperses

Whether guiding the people of Israel through the wilderness (Exod. 13:21), leading Jesus into the desert (Matt. 4:1), or prompting the apostles to bear witness to the gospel in "Jerusalem, and in all Judea and Samaria, and to the farthest parts of the earth" (Acts

31. Richard Beck, *The Slavery of Death* (Eugene, OR: Cascade Books, 2013), 70. Here Beck is quoting from Arthur C. McGill, *Death and Life: An American Theology* (Eugene, OR: Wipf & Stock, 2003), 49–50.

1:8), the Spirit of God not only animates, disrupts, and decenters, but disperses the human spirit as well. This kind of scattering is another form of disruption, but its principal orientation is outward (toward the world) rather than inward (toward the self). This is to say, as *hevel* gives way to *ruach*, the Spirit of God moves us into places and spaces that, if we're being honest, we would likely never have chosen ourselves. To be sure, this kind of movement is almost always uncomfortable, in large part because it is quite literally an unsettling. But that's just what it means to be inspired or, better yet, in-spirited. It is to join in with the movement of the Divine Breath of Life that cannot be contained or coerced and, in many cases, is thoroughly unpredictable. As Jesus would remind us, "The wind blows wherever it will, and you hear the sound it makes, but do not know where it comes from and where it is going. So it is with everyone who is born of the Spirit" (John 3:8).

As the risk-averse creatures that we are, we tend to shy away from such unpredictability in favor of something more certain and reliable. But this resistance to the unknown merely exposes how stagnant and settled we've become, how prone we are to retreating into the safety and comfort of the known. Thus, to participate with the Spirit as Jesus, the apostles, and the people of Israel once did is not to avoid or run away from being radically unsettled. It is to run headlong into an unpredictable future filled with equal parts risk and excitement, knowing full well that the Spirit of God will be present with us, ushering us into places that we could never have asked for or imagined (Eph. 3:20) and, in doing so, transforming us.

Cultivating Space Where *Ruach* and *Hevel* Meet

As theologically imaginative as all this talk of the Spirit as the breath of life may be, some may be wondering what exactly this has to do with John, the young man we met earlier who is seeking professional help for his mental health. From a theological perspective, what does it mean for a person like John to experience healing, growth, or transformation if he never comes to a saving knowledge of Christ? Doesn't the entire Christian tradition hinge on the confession of the resurrected Christ as humanity's only true hope for healing and restoration? If so, can we really speak of John's life being renewed, much less him flourishing, if Christ's redemptive work is never even considered? As Ezekiel 18:23 points out, it pleases God even when the wicked turn from their destructive patterns of death and instead choose life, so surely the same is true for a person like John. At the very least, God desires for John to experience a life of wholeness and well-being because John, like every human, is part of God's good creation. But is that all we can say? Could it be that, perhaps, the Spirit of God is not merely pleased with John's journey but is in fact actively and passionately involved in his life as the source of his healing, whether explicitly acknowledged or not?

Others may have more general concerns, wondering how this notion of the Spirit ought to inform our understanding of the ways in which humans are able to collaborate with God's activity in any domain (e.g., the therapeutic context) that is not explicitly Christian, religious, or even theistic. Given that people really do get better in therapy, how do we make sense of this as Christians, especially when it involves people who are not Christians and Christ is never mentioned? In the next chapter, we will examine the relational dimension of these questions, considering more fully the ways in which healing happens in and through relationships. But we will also take up these questions in more depth and detail in part 2 of the book, where we will explore the various ways in which the Spirit's work impacts and, in a very real sense, makes possible the work that takes place in the context of psychotherapy.

For now, building on the image of a dissipated mist, it will be enough to say that to participate with the Spirit of God is simply to have the courage to enter the space where *ruach* and *hevel* meet, allowing our human spirit to give way to the Spirit of God. In these spaces, our task is not to exert control over the chaos of our lives or the lives of others. Our task is simply to submit to a force at work in the world that not only energizes and in-spirits us but also disrupts, scatters, and undoes us. As the biblical testimony makes clear, this process can be as unsettling as it is inspiring, and it almost always moves us in surprising and unexpected ways.

Yet, beyond a simple willingness to enter a potentially disruptive space, a robust pneumatology like the one we have outlined suggests that the primary objective for the student of psychology is to focus on developing their skills at *creating* such spaces—growing in their capacity to cultivate environments where they and their clients can together inhale and exhale God's life-giving breath.[32] To underscore the level of humility required for this endeavor, it is important to keep in mind that the divine *ruach* is always already blowing in and through our client's lives. So our role in curating these spaces has almost nothing to do with leveraging our power or resources or ingenuity; rather, it's about joining in the divine movement that was already in motion long before we joined in and will continue long after our contributions come to an end.

In this regard, we appreciate Moltmann's perspective. For Moltmann, *ruach* is not only a personal presence but also the transcendent space in which we live "in" God's Spirit. Just as God provides the psalmist the ability to stand out of harm's way in "a wide open place" (Ps. 31:8), we experience the presence of God's *ruach* as the space in which we "live and move and have our being" (Acts 17:28 NRSV). In this space, *ruach* is the most silent and hidden presence of God's Spirit, for it is both in us and around us. Ultimately then, for us to collaborate with God's *ruach* is to cultivate spaces where we do not simply talk *about* the Spirit, but where we talk *out of* the Spirit.[33] In other words, it is to create space where we can come together in unexpected places, forge unexpected friendships, and simply breathe.

32. Megan Anna Neff echoes this sentiment when she recounts an experience she had with one of her clients:

> My work with Brooke was humbling and awe provoking in that I quickly realized I was just one piece of *the work God was already up to in her life*. . . . There is no sophisticated model for integration at play here; what I needed to do with Brooke *was simply to create a space* of acceptance that allowed for God's presence while having ears to hear when she talked about her spiritual life. God was with us in the therapy room each week, and God continued to be with Brooke in the intervening times through her relationships, in church, in nature, and through prayer. (Neff and McMinn, *Embodying Integration,* 180, emphasis added)

33. Moltmann, *Spirit of Life,* 57.

Questions for Reflection and Discussion

1. How have pastors, parents, and other Christian leaders in your life addressed the biblical passages referenced in this chapter (if at all)? Has our discussion of these passages changed the way you understand God's broader work in the world?

2. If the Spirit of God is to humans what an author is to the fictional characters in a novel, what does this mean for the various projects we pursue (psychological or otherwise)?

3. How does the image of *ruach* and *hevel* support or challenge your understanding of God's involvement in your life's work?

4. What would it look like, in concrete terms, for you to participate in the Spirit's work of animation, disruption, decentering, and dispersal?

Resources for Reading and Exploration

Beck, Richard. *The Slavery of Death*. Eugene, OR: Cascade Books, 2014.

Johnston, Robert K. *God's Wider Presence: Reconsidering General Revelation*. Grand Rapids: Baker Academic, 2014.

Pargament, Kenneth I. *Spiritually Integrated Psychotherapy: Understanding and Addressing the Sacred*. New York: Guilford Press, 2007.

4

Christology, Incarnation, and the *Imago Dei*

Key takeaways from this chapter:

- The fullest manifestation of God's incarnational project is the person and work of Jesus.
- Jesus's incarnation is the means by which God is redeeming all aspects of human life, including our bodies and emotions.
- Christ's entering into the suffering and pain of others gives us a glimpse of what an incarnational psychology might look like.
- Being human is not a destination but a journey in which we become more like Christ, the *imago Dei*.

I (William) had the good fortune one day to be driving in my car while Krista Tippet's wonderful radio program, *On Being*, was being broadcast on NPR. On this day, Krista had just started interviewing the well-known Quaker author and educator Parker Palmer. Palmer was describing his experience with depression and how difficult it was during that time for people to sit and be with him in his depressive state. Here is his recollection:

> These were the people who would say, "Gosh, Parker, why are you sitting in here being depressed? It's a beautiful day outside. Go feel the sunshine and smell the flowers." And that, of course, leaves a depressed person even more depressed, because while you know, intellectually, that it's sunny out and that the flowers are lovely and fragrant, you can't really feel any of that in your body, which is dead in a sensory way. And so you're left more depressed by this "good advice" to get out and enjoy the day. And then other people would come and say something along the lines of "Gosh, Parker, why are you depressed? You're such a good person. . . . You're so successful, and you've written so well." And that would leave me feeling more depressed because I would feel, "I've just defrauded another person who, if they really knew what a schmuck I was, would cast me into the darkness where I already am."[1]

Those of you who have struggled with depression might know exactly what Palmer is describing. Having gone through my own battle with depression in my twenties, I (William) can relate to the hopelessness and deadness of the feeling Palmer described, and I can also attest to how frustrating it was being offered quick-fix solutions from well-intentioned people. Frankly, church leaders can sometimes lead the pack in advice-giving, providing spiritual solutions wrapped up in tidy little packages like "pray more" or "cast your cares upon God." It's not that this advice has no kernel of truth in it, but it's especially misguided when it is offered from a place where the person giving the advice is doing so because they are uncomfortable sitting with the person who is suffering. But even if depression isn't something that you've experienced firsthand, you probably can still relate to a time when you've been in pain or have been suffering. Instead of a friend or family member seeking to try to understand your experience, listen to you, or be present with you, they tried to

---

1. *On Being* with Krista Tippett, "The Soul in Depression," interview with Parker Palmer, original air date January 17, 2003, available at https://onbeing.org/programs /the-soul-in-depression/.

"fix" the problem as they understood it, or gave you advice on what you needed to do. As the program continued, Palmer went on:

> There was this one friend who . . . after asking permission to do so, every afternoon about 4 o'clock, sat me down in a chair in the living room, took off my shoes and socks, and massaged my feet. He hardly ever said anything; he was a Quaker elder. And yet, out of his intuitive sense, from time to time would say a very brief word like, "I can feel your struggle today," or, farther down the road, "I feel that you're a little stronger at this moment, and I'm glad for that." But beyond that, he would hardly say anything. He would give no advice. He would simply report, from time to time, what he was intuiting about my condition. Somehow he found the one place in my body, namely the soles of my feet, where I could experience some sort of connection to another human being. And the act of massaging just—in a way that I really don't have words for—kept me connected with the human race.[2]

Palmer's story provides a beautiful picture of what it means to have someone sit and be present with suffering, staying connected with another human being. What Palmer did not need were people trying to offer advice. What was most helpful was having a person making a connection with him in a very tactile and bodily way. Parker's friend offered help and comfort that was "incarnated" in a particular way through bodily presence and empathy. As Palmer relates, this friend was also willing to hold the "sacred space of relationship" for him.[3]

What Palmer describes as a sacred space connects to some of the main themes that we will discuss in this chapter: incarnation, embodiment, and restoration. As we look at the ministry and mystery of the incarnation—that is, God becoming flesh in Jesus Christ—we find the origin of what it truly means to enter the world of another.

Christ entered into the suffering of the human world, giving precedent for what it means to enter into the suffering of others. Thus, the main purpose of this chapter is to consider what it means for us to practice psychology in light of the Christian belief that God has been revealed in Jesus Christ. A closely related concern has to do with how our psychological research and clinical practice might be

---

2. *On Being* with Krista Tippett, "The Soul in Depression."
3. *On Being* with Krista Tippett, "The Soul in Depression."

different (and perhaps should be different) given that we believe that humans are created in the image of the God who took on flesh. This theological framework paints a picture of what an "incarnational" psychology might look like. While this topic could be a book all on its own, for now we want to orient you to a number of key areas regarding the ongoing work of Christ, expound on what it means for human beings to be created in the image of God, and then discuss a few of the ways these theological concepts overlap with topics in psychology.

In the previous chapter, we talked about how the presence of God's Spirit is vital for recognizing and affirming the ways humans can partner with God's activity in the broader world, and how this includes realms that are not explicitly Christian, or even theistic. We've also turned to the doctrine of creation as a foundational theological doctrine for conceptualizing the relationship between psychology and the Christian faith, providing the "stage" where God's action in the world takes place through the Son and Spirit. Along similar lines, Irenaeus used the metaphor of God's "two hands" in the world as the working of the Son and Spirit.[4] And it is a trinitarian framework of precisely this kind that provides a starting point for how we talk about the significance of the Son's and the Spirit's work in the church and the broader world. To speak of God as Trinity— God as Father, Son, and Spirit—is to make a statement about the relational nature of God. Or, said another way, God exists in relationship and invites the world and the human creature into the joy and abundance of God's own life through Jesus Christ. Ultimately, God's action of creating, sustaining, redeeming, and perfecting the world and humanity through the Son and Spirit is the gospel story, a story of love. As such, it is also the lens through which we understand the world around us, ourselves, and, as it relates to our present purposes, even psychology.

4. Marianne Meye Thompson observes that one of the best explanations of the "unity of Father, Son and Spirit is Irenaeus's characterization of the Son and Spirit, Word and Wisdom, as the 'two hands of God' which highlights that the actual agency in the whole of salvation history, both creation and redemption and all that lies between, really is rooted in the Father." "The Raising of Lazarus in John 11," in *The Gospel of John in Christian Theology*, ed. Richard Bauckham and Carl Mosser (Grand Rapids: Eerdmans, 2008), 26.

God *creates* and brings the human creature into existence out of love. God *sustains* the human creature through the Spirit (despite humanity's refusal to sometimes participate in the action of God). God *redeems* the human creature through Christ. And God *perfects* the human creature over time by bringing the Creator's original intentions to fulfillment through the Spirit of Christ. As we discussed in chapters 2 and 3, it is possible to understand human involvement in clinical and research psychology as God's Spirit actively calling and enabling human creatures to participate as co-laborers in God's creative work to bring about wholeness and healing. In this chapter, we direct our attention more closely to the ways that God's revelation, incarnation, and redemption through Jesus Christ make a difference for understanding aspects of human flourishing, the affirmation of our emotional and bodily states, and the possibility of liberation from oppression.

God's Revelation in Jesus Christ

The bulk of the previous chapter was about how people of Christian faith would benefit from thinking of general revelation in terms of God's wider presence, which includes the work of the Spirit within creation, conscience, and human culture (and this includes realms of psychology). Here we will focus more on what theologians have historically spoken of as special revelation, which is God's revelation and salvation through Jesus Christ. In some ways the terms "general revelation" and "special revelation" are helpful, especially when delineating the uniqueness of Christ's life, death, and resurrection. While general revelation provides glimpses of God's goodness, beauty, and truth to the world, it does not detail or give specifics of salvation through Jesus Christ. However, in other ways the terms "general" and "special" revelation are unhelpful, especially when we forget that general and special revelation work together as complementary modes of God's loving extension into the world through the Spirit and Son. God's revelatory presence sustains and protects creation, allowing humans to discover truths through the sciences and psychology that are reliable and trustworthy (general revelation). At the same time, God's self-disclosure also restores and redeems humanity (special revelation). Having described some of the ways God's wider presence manifests through general revelation, here we hope to demonstrate some of the contours of special revelation that directly affect our work in the psychological sciences.

The central message of the Christian faith is that God reveals God's own self through Jesus. This confession is so comprehensive (even cosmic) in its scope that it impacts every topic we explore and every discipline in which we participate, including psychology. The Christian church through the centuries has reflected on this confession of Christ within the varied contexts and cultures that the church has found itself. In certain important respects, just as we indicated in chapter 3, the Christian confession that Christ is Lord moves us beyond the walls of the church, inviting us to imagine how Christ's work makes a difference for the societies, cultures, and neighborhoods in which we live and work. We also suggested in chapter 1 that psychology is its own culture (albeit a scientific one) with a set of practices, languages, institutions, and traditions that constitute it as such. The task then for Christians who work within psychology is to begin to contextualize how the person and work of Christ makes a difference for the various fields of psychology they find themselves in.

When we think about the difference that Christ makes for the field of psychology, we are engaging in the same task that Christians have engaged throughout history as they considered how God might be made "incarnate" within their own contexts and cultures, each of which was as wide-ranging as it was particular. Moreover, when we think about Christ becoming flesh in order to redeem and restore, this has numerous implications for how we understand the flourishing or thriving of the human creature. Confession of Christ involves a proper (re)ordering of our lives and actions, and the centrality of Christ's life and work impacts the vocation that we have been called to, no matter what that work looks like or what that discipline might be. Whether it involves helping to guide and transform the relationships and behavioral patterns of a child, adolescent, or family as a psychotherapist, or conducting ethical psychological research in any subdiscipline as a psychological scientist, our confession of Christ impacts and shapes our day-to-day work, our ethical vision, and our sense of vocation as psychological practitioners.

Incarnation, Abundant Life, and Shalom

Christians who study psychology can understand Christ's work of salvation as an affirmation that Christ came to restore and redeem *all aspects* of human existence—that is, the bodily, the spiritual, and the emotional. Jesus experienced the full range of human emotions, living a life of joyful intimacy and communion with God and others. This does not mean that Jesus did not suffer, experience sadness, or have anguish, as he most certainly did (see Matt. 26:38; Luke 22:44). In fact, Jesus encountered moments of profound grief (John 11:35) and even anger (Mark 3:1–6; John 2:15–17). What we learn from Jesus is that to experience life as a human is to be present and feel and experience the joy and struggles of the world in which we live. To be human also means that we live in a world where God's kingdom has partially come but is not fully actualized. Sadness, anger, and suffering are realities that we could not completely eliminate. Like Jesus, Christians still hurt (and unfortunately, hurt others too). Those who follow Christ still encounter suffering, and they still have to work through family and relational conflict. As Parker Palmer states, "To move close to God is to move close to everything that human beings have ever experienced . . . and that, of course, includes a lot of suffering, as well as a lot of joy."[5] This reality alone can ground and center us as we also encounter suffering or stand alongside those who suffer (2 Cor. 1:4–5; Heb. 2:18).

The message of the gospel is that, in Christ, God's kingdom has broken into the world in a new way, but one that still waits eagerly for complete restoration. God is not a dispassionate observer of our suffering, though. We can affirm as Christians that we have a God who suffered in Christ. Furthermore, God does not abandon us in our suffering. According to the New Testament, rather than offering a purely "spiritual" solution for the concrete problems that plague humanity, the abundant life that Christ offers includes bodily restoration, proclamation of freedom for those imprisoned, recovery of sight for the blind, and freedom for those who are oppressed (Luke 4:18). These movements of redemption and healing caused theologians Elisabeth Moltmann-Wendell and Jürgen Moltmann to sum

5. *On Being* with Krista Tippett, "The Soul in Depression."

them up as the "great love story of the Father, the Son, and the Holy Spirit, a divine love story in which we are all involved together with heaven and earth."[6] Though sin distorts how humanity relates to God and hinders human flourishing and disrupts the created order, it does not corrupt creation entirely or alter God's commitment to the human community through the Son and Spirit.[7] God's covenant love continues to graciously sustain humanity and to "overrule the worst that the human race can do to subvert [God's] order."[8]

Wholeness, restoration, new life, abundant life, harmony, peace, shalom: these are all words that attempt to capture elements of the human flourishing that Christ actualizes through his incarnation, life, death, and resurrection. The Hebrew word "shalom," however, offers a particularly rich and meaningful description of the abundant life that Jesus brings. It is often translated as "peace," but a fuller examination of the word describes more than just an absence of conflict; it also connotes wholeness and abundance of life. Cornelius Plantinga describes shalom as the "webbing together of God, humans, and all creation in justice, fulfillment, and delight."[9] Shalom is the way God intends things to be, where God's justice and peace reign supreme, where relationships are ordered toward love instead of toward greed, hate, or violence. Shalom is a glimpse of a new reality where the wolf and the lamb will dwell together and all creation will not hurt or destroy one another (Isa. 11:6–10). Shalom gives us a vision of a reality where humans properly understand their place in the cosmos—not existing to dominate or destroy creation or others but to tend and care for the things God has placed under human supervision.

Frankly, who doesn't want a world where more peace, mercy, and love reign supreme? Who doesn't long for the day when justice rolls down like a river, and righteousness like a mighty stream (Amos 5:24)? The vision of wholeness and flourishing captured by shalom is one

6. Elisabeth Moltmann-Wendell and Jürgen Moltmann, *Humanity in God* (New York: Pilgrim Press, 1983), 88.

7. Jürgen Moltmann, *God in Creation: A New Theology of Creation and the Spirit of God*, trans. Margeret Kohl (Minneapolis: Fortress, 1985).

8. Colin E. Gunton, *The Triune Creator: A Historical and Systematic Study* (Grand Rapids: Eerdmans, 1988), 192.

9. Cornelius Plantinga, *Not the Way It's Supposed to Be: A Breviary on Sin* (Grand Rapids: Eerdmans, 1995), 10.

that almost everyone can agree would be good and shares a longing in their hearts for. As students of psychology, we imagine there is a longing for something like shalom in your own heart as you pursue psychological training in order to help others find peace through mental health. Following this core desire is an important part of incarnating the love of Christ and working toward shalom in your own corner of the world, through your work, calling, life, and vocation.

Jesus brought a foretaste of this shalom to humanity through his life, death, and resurrection. The prospering and flourishing of human life is what Jesus's ministry of reconciliation is about, and longing for God's kingdom here on earth means becoming Christ incarnate to those we serve as we cultivate shalom in the arenas that God has given us. God's work through the Spirit and Son is the movement to restore and redeem a creation that has been disrupted by sin. Shalom is the wholeness that God intended for human and nonhuman creation. Balanced with an understanding of the doctrine of creation and pneumatology (explored in chaps. 2 and 3), the concept of shalom makes clear that students of psychology who are people of Christian faith have a role in tending, caring for, and being good stewards of the small part of the created realm they inhabit.[10]

Incarnation and Embodiment as an Affirmation of Bodily Existence

All Christian theology hinges on the fact that God became flesh in Jesus Christ to bring restoration to the world. Because God's project in the world is incarnational (i.e., enfleshed), it brings about a holistic form of restoration that includes all aspects of human existence (the bodily, mental, and emotional realms of human personhood). Although not every dimension of human existence will be restored in the present life, it can begin in the here and now and will be brought to completion in the age to come (the eschaton). For example, the cognitive and emotional development of human persons and their learned patterns of behavior, which are distinctly psychological phenomena,

10. William Whitney, "Beginnings: Why the Doctrine of Creation Matters for the Integration of Psychology and Christianity," *Journal of Psychology and Theology* 48, no. 1 (2020): 61.

are the very realms that are impacted by the abundant life that Jesus describes in John 10:10. These psychological processes may not be fully restored in the present age, but they can be integrated into our lives in ways that promote rather than preclude the cultivation of shalom, or wholeness.

To move in the direction of this kind of wholeness, however, we must first and foremost acknowledge that human life is both physical and embodied. Warren Brown and Brad Strawn helpfully remind us that, as humans, we do not merely *have* bodies but we *are* embodied creatures, and there is no reality that we encounter that can be perceived apart from our own physicality.[11] Because God has created a world where human life is both physical and embodied, God's redemptive work in the world also involves God becoming incarnated in bodily form in Jesus Christ.[12] God's saving, restoration, and healing are embodied in Jesus Christ. This fact alone highlights the value of us being created as material and bodily beings. Jesus's incarnation offers an important affirmation of both human and nonhuman creation. Indeed, according to Irenaeus, the incarnation alone is the basis for God's affirmation of the goodness of the material world and bodily existence. Irenaeus reasoned that if God the Son takes the form of human flesh, then nothing that is created can be downgraded as unimportant or be treated as fundamentally evil.[13]

Jesus's human bodily existence, his experience of the full range of emotional states, and his encounters with suffering demonstrate the value of the human experience, which includes both our bodily existence and our various emotional and psychological states. Thus, the doctrine of the incarnation provides the theological basis for much of the work that we do in the field of psychology, especially as it relates to the affirmation of human life, emotions, and relationships, but also as it concerns the validation of the suffering and pain

---

11. Warren S. Brown and Brad D. Strawn, *The Physical Nature of Christian Life: Neuroscience, Psychology, and the Church* (New York: Cambridge University Press, 2012), 16.

12. William A. Dyrness, *The Earth Is God's: A Theology of American Culture* (Maryknoll, NY: Orbis Books, 1997), 20.

13. These insights from Irenaeus are mentioned in Gunton, *Triune Creator*, 52.

that we as humans encounter. Of course, as we discussed before, certain aspects of our bodily existence and our psychosocial life are also affirmed through the doctrine of creation. In addition to God's incarnation in Jesus, the very fact that God freely created the world out of love is itself the ultimate affirmation of creation's goodness. God is the one who loves in freedom, freely creates the world out of love, and freely creates because love seeks to share its goodness.[14]

As a consequence, God's disclosure of God's own self through the Son and Spirit serves as the larger theological framework not only for understanding our own embodied lives but also for how our lives are transformed through the person and work of Christ. God's creative project in the world has an ultimate end or aim (telos), which is to sustain, redeem, and bring wholeness to humanity (and the entire creation). Jesus comes to restore human life and existence, and he provides the perfect example of how a human creature's relationships, emotions, and mind have the potential for being shaped toward the telos that God has intended. And one particular way in which Christ reshapes the telos of human existence is by demonstrating what it looks like to live under the guidance and direction of the Spirit on a moment-by-moment basis (Gal. 5:25).

God's incarnation in Jesus Christ is therefore a testament both to God's compassionate love for a world that is "very good" (Gen. 1:31) and to God's desire for the human creature to be directed toward ends that are equally good. That being said, to affirm that the nonhuman world (animals, plants, soil, oceans) and the human creature are good is not to deny the reality of evil. We must always acknowledge that the reality of evil remains a threat that impinges on God's good creation, but we can affirm that God calls creation good in the beginning and that Jesus becoming flesh through the incarnation further affirms that humans, in their emotions, physicality, and biology, are not inherently bad or evil. This is good news for us who study psychology, since so much psychological research is concerned with the very basic emotional, bodily, and behavioral aspects of human existence.

14. Karl Barth, *Church Dogmatics* II/1, trans. G. W. Bromiley (Edinburgh, Scotland: T&T Clark, 1961), 257.

Motivated by this theological vision, it follows that at least some aspects of human healing and wholeness can be aided and guided by the discipline of psychology. This does not mean that psychology, the sciences writ large, or some theory of psychotherapy could ever replace the salvation and restoration offered in Christ. However, the argument we want to put forward is that affirming the centrality of our emotional and bodily life is more critical than ever given the Christian tradition's historical tendency to elevate the spiritual realm while simultaneously devaluing the body and emotions. Within evangelical and fundamentalist streams of Christianity in particular, the decoupling of the human creature from the human body has led to forms of mission that stress the salvation of one's soul to the neglect of the bodily needs of human existence (e.g., disregarding necessities such as food, shelter, clothing). Here, Protestants can learn much from their Catholic sisters and brothers, whose lived theology has often held the church's mission of salvation, human dignity, and social justice together in a much tighter way than some streams of White Protestant Christianity in the twentieth century.[15]

To say that aspects of wholeness and healing can be aided by psychology is to recognize that restoration is often transmitted or mediated in a relational and bodily form, and that psychotherapists often act as an embodied (and incarnated) form of love for their clients or patients. It is also to recognize that, through the creation of these hospitable spaces, healing can and does occur. Our ability to shape, tend, and nurture the created realm is directly related to the ways in which we cultivate our human relations as well. Relationships that are tended and nurtured through love over time have the potential to thrive, and those relationships that have been neglected and shaped by hatred, violence, or greed lead to a diminishment rather than an enhancement of human personhood. Our actions and speech have creative capacities, and while we are finite creatures who do not create life out of nothing (*ex nihilo*), we do shape relational realms through our actions and speech, each of which has the potential for producing either the restoration or diminishment of life.

15. George Marsden, *Fundamentalism and American Culture*, 2nd ed. (New York: Oxford University Press, 2006), 229–58.

Christ in Varied Contexts: Liberation from Stigmatization and Discrimination

In the first chapter we talked about how both psychology and theology represent different traditions of inquiry. We also discussed the various lenses that theologians have commonly looked through in order to gain clarity on their lives and the world. Just as we noted that there are different lenses that theologians use, we also noted that, within the Protestant Christian tradition, there are also varied denominational and cultural lenses that give us a rich diversity of views and interpretations of Scripture. We all read Scripture from a situated standpoint—a sociocultural context in which we are embedded. As a result, we interpret the person and work of Christ through the lenses provided to us by our family, background, culture, and community of faith. As theologian Daniel Migliore notes, traditional Western (and predominantly White) interpretations of the person and work of Christ are no less contextual than those done by Black theologians or those of women.[16] In short, cultural history, tradition, and context also influence the various ways that we understand Christ's work of salvation and restoration. Examining how Christ has been understood in varied cultural contexts provides essential elements for understanding the person and work of Christ, especially in relation to Christ's ministry of restoration and reconciliation. This is an important point to highlight because White, Western, Protestant, evangelical conceptions of Christ have often conceptualized salvation as an entirely "otherworldly" process. In doing so, they overlook the significance of emotional and psychological states, failing to recognize that salvation cannot be separated from the concrete realities that constitute human life in the created order.

Responding in part to these historic oversights, David Kelsey's *Eccentric Existence* argues that we should understand theological anthropology in both proximate and ultimate arenas. "Proximate" arenas of existence and restoration are those that relate to the immediate physical, social, and cultural lives of humans. "Ultimate" arenas of existence and restoration are those that are primarily in

---

16. Daniel L. Migliore, *Faith Seeking Understanding: An Introduction to Christian Theology* (Grand Rapids: Eerdmans, 2004), 187.

relation to God, salvation, and the cosmos.[17] According to Kelsey, Christologies developed by African Americans, Latinx, female, and Asian American theologians, as well as theologies constructed by persons of color, tend to emphasize these proximate arenas of human existence in ways that are applied and oriented toward justice. To focus on these proximate realms is to consider how various forms of oppression, systemic injustices, and the diminishment of human existence are brought about by racism, poverty, and sexism. Each of these serves as a key element for any contemporary theological reflection, but they become even more pertinent as we consider the relations between psychology and Christianity. Let us consider a few of the ways in which constructive theologies that emphasize these proximate arenas might help us understand more fully how we can engage in theologically informed psychology.

Liberation Theologies

A deep and abiding concern for social justice often serves as one of the primary motivations for much of the work that we do in psychology. As both of us (William and Kutter) think back to the time we studied at the Fuller Graduate School of Psychology, we remember many classmates who wanted to become psychologists almost entirely because of their desire to help underserved populations, to seek justice in systems that are oppressive, or to provide mental health services for communities where there are pronounced disparities in the health-care system. The emphasis that Christianity places on the dignity of every human life as a beloved child of God, whether poor or rich, whether Black, Brown, or White, is a vital feature of the gospel. Liberation theology in particular has drawn attention to the important fact that Christians should be very concerned with the plight of the poor. Given that the poor, underprivileged, and marginalized in contemporary societies not only have access to fewer resources but are also oppressed by systems and structures that often favor the rich and those with privilege and power, liberation theology reminds us that, as Christians, we have an obligation

17. David H. Kelsey, *Eccentric Existence: A Theological Anthropology*, 2 vols. (Louisville: Westminster John Knox, 2009), 1:4–5.

to pursue justice for "the least of these" (Matt. 25:40). Liberation theology's notion that the church should have a preferential option for the poor is informed by readings of the gospel that understand Jesus as being part of a marginalized group living primarily among the poor.[18] For Latin American theologians, Jesus not only identified with those who were on the margins of society but also confronted sinful systems of oppression that kept people in bondage. Our understanding of a theologically engaged psychology is informed by the basic principles espoused by liberation theologians that move us to understand Christ's work as being involved in these proximate areas of societal injustices in relation to the poor.

Black Theology, Feminist Theology

While liberation theologies and Latin American theologians draw attention to the plight of the poor and systems of oppression, Black theologians rightly draw attention to the complexities and systemic injustices perpetrated by the racist structures of contemporary society. Feminist and womanist theologians draw our attention to sexist structures of society that overlook women, and especially women of color.

One of the chief architects of contemporary Black theology, James Cone, puts it like this: "The gospel of Jesus is not a rational concept to be explained in a theory of salvation, but a story about God's presence in Jesus' solidarity with the oppressed, which led to his death on the cross. What is redemptive is the fact that God snatches victory out of defeat, life out of death, and hope out of despair. . . . I begin and end my theological reflections in the social context of Black people's struggle for justice."[19]

---

18. Liberation theology was popularized by Gustavo Gutiérrez, *A Theology of Liberation* (Maryknoll, NY: Orbis Books, 1973). Liberation theology's followers and ideologies have had a rocky relationship with the official Catholic Church until more recently, when Pope Francis, the first Latin American pope, indicated that the church should have preference for the poor, going so far as to call for a "poor church for the poor." See "Pope Francis Wants 'Poor Church for the Poor,'" BBC News, March 16, 2013, https://www.bbc.com/news/world-europe-21812545.

19. James H. Cone, *The Cross and the Lynching Tree* (Maryknoll, NY: Orbis Books, 2011), 150–51.

Black theology was born out of the experiences of those within North America who have struggled against the oppression of racism and the brutal legacy of slavery. Cone reminds us that God's salvation is a liberating event in the lives of all who are struggling for survival and dignity in a world bent on denying their humanity.[20] Moreover, Black theologians remind us that the cross has a unique meaning for those who are currently experiencing oppression and suffering. As Howard Thurman explains, "It cannot be denied that too often the weight of the Christian movement has been on the side of the strong and the powerful and against the weak and oppressed—this, despite the gospel."[21] Thus, the basic message that Jesus stands in solidarity with the poor, with those who experience racism, and with those who experience exploitation by an oppressive system is often missed by those in positions of privilege who have not experienced racism, slavery, or living under an oppressive system. Black theologians remind us that context and race matter for how we read and interpret Scripture. For instance, a middle-class White male who reads Luke 4 about Jesus bringing freedom for captives and those who are oppressed might envision those who are physically in the prison system, and he might even have some thoughts of what it would mean to serve those who are incarcerated. However, Black theologians remind us that when a Black woman or man reads about freedom for the oppressed and the captive in a passage like Luke 4, they might remember the historic system of chattel slavery that imprisoned and oppressed grandparents or great-grandparents, or recall the ongoing inequity in our prison system where persons of color regularly receive longer and more severe sentences for the same crimes compared to their White counterparts.[22] As Danté Stewart notes, "To be black and to be Christian is to remember the brutality of our experience and the brilliance of our resistance."[23]

20. Cone, *The Cross and the Lynching Tree*, 151.

21. Howard Thurman, *Jesus and the Disinherited* (Boston: Beacon, 1996), 31.

22. Christopher Ingraham, "Black Men Sentenced to More Time for Committing the Exact Same Crime as a White Person, Study Finds," *Washington Post*, Nov. 16, 2017, https://www.washingtonpost.com/news/wonk/wp/2017/11/16/black-men-sentenced-to-more-time-for-committing-the-exact-same-crime-as-a-white-person-study-finds.

23. Danté Stewart, "Black Theology Sings of Freedom," *Christianity Today*, Feb. 25, 2020, https://www.christianitytoday.com/ct/2020/february-web-only/black-theology-sings-freedom-dante-stewart.html.

Along with the ideas found in liberation and Black theologies concerning Jesus's solidarity with the oppressed, feminist theologians similarly note that their theology of the cross is informed by their experience of being excluded or oppressed because of their gender. To be a feminist, according to theologian Anne Carr, is to be "someone (male or female) who recognizes that women are fully human, acknowledges the imbalance and injustice that for centuries has, in church and society, characterized the situation of women, and is committed to righting that wrong."[24] Feminist theologies (typically those done by White women), womanist theologies (feminist theological perspectives by Black women), and *mujerista* theologies (feminist theological perspectives from Hispanic and Latinx women) all alert us to how oppressive systems of patriarchy and toxic masculinity (and, yes, these are particularly found within the church) can lead to a devaluing and subjugation of women. As feminist theologians correctly point out, Jesus's identification with those on the margins provides the basis for paying particular attention to the plight of women, since women have for centuries found themselves on the margins of society and the church. New Testament feminist scholars emphasize that the movement Jesus initiated was fundamentally egalitarian, or "at least was a countercultural movement that leveled class, ethnic and gender differences, and one that heralded 'a new redemptive humanity.'"[25]

As Christians, when we consider what it means to stand in solidarity with the poor, the oppressed, the marginalized, and those who have felt the ostracizing effects of racism or sexism, we understand that our work in psychology must bend toward social justice as well. When we take seriously the fact that Jesus was poor, lived under an oppressive Roman regime, and preached to and healed those who were on the margins, we have no other choice but to examine our own privileges and to work to increase the welfare and flourishing of others. If Jesus Christ is only thought of as a spiritual being, detached from his incarnate, cultural, and embodied humanity, we risk

24. Anne Carr, "Feminist Views of Christology," *Chicago Studies* 35 (August 1996): 128.
25. Lisa Isherwood and Dorothea McEwan, eds., *An A to Z of Feminist Theology* (Sheffield: Sheffield Academic, 1996), 26.

not only overlooking God's preferential option for the marginalized and the poor, but also projecting our own cultural values onto Jesus.[26]

Consequently, when we speak of the "reality of the gospel," we specifically mean a robust vision of humanity and salvation that properly incorporates movement toward others. Theologian Colin Gunton puts it this way: "If Jesus is the one true image of God, and is the one in whom the right dominion of the creation is re-established as he speaks of truth, heals the sick and lifts up the oppressed," then it follows that those who desire to make Christ "incarnate" for the world will find themselves doing many of the same things.[27] This movement is grounded in our vocation within psychology and includes actively *shaping social realities* for the kingdom. It is true that redemption is about restoration from individual sin, but this also means that we work for redemption on a societal and communal level—working to redeem culturally and socially ingrained imaginations and values. Christ's incarnation inaugurated a new kingdom and established him as the model for how to treat people with dignity and live in harmony.

On a systemic level, liberation, Black, and feminist theologies remind us of the disheartening and unsettling fact that the church can house prejudices and engage in oppressive behavior toward those with different ethnic heritages and social statuses, just like our wider culture can. For instance, we recall the disturbing reality that many White slaveholders during the 1800s also professed to be Christians. Moreover, when we zoom in on the individual level, disciplines like neuropsychology and cognitive psychology reveal how malleable and plastic our decision-making is—even for Christians. This research suggests that when one is in extremely stressful situations, executive functions are diminished, decision-making is altered, and underlying habitual responses take over.[28] It is a humbling reminder that Christians *are* influenced by power structures and society's dominant

26. J. Kameron Carter, *Race: A Theological Account* (Oxford: Oxford University Press, 2008).

27. Gunton, *Triune Creator*, 210.

28. See Amy F. T. Arnsten, "Stress Signaling Pathways That Impair Prefrontal Cortex Structure and Function," *Nature Reviews Neuroscience* 10, no. 6 (2009): 410–22; and L. Schwabe and O. T. Wolf, "Stress and Multiple Memory Systems: From 'Thinking' to 'Doing,'" *Trends in Cognitive Sciences* 17, no. 2 (2013): 60–68.

worldview. As a consequence, we have the potential to act in accordance with learned stereotypes that can oppress others, unless these are actively considered, countered, and changed. To be more specific, events that have shaped our conscience—like officer-involved killings of unarmed Black men and women—are not isolated events, and they remind us of the history of systemic oppression, injustice, and racism that have had, and continue to have, devastating effects on the children of God. Many racist events have been dismissed by White Christians, instead of calling out evil for what it is. One is reminded of Martin Luther King Jr.'s incisive observation: "We will have to repent in this generation not merely for the hateful words and actions of the bad people but for the appalling silence of the good people."[29]

Yet, we do not have to settle for this kind of silence. Christ's example of standing in solidarity with the oppressed provides us with a vision to follow in working to dismantle our own racist and oppressive thoughts and behaviors. As authors, we believe this cannot be done unless we practice an incarnational psychology and enter into the reality of another—not through seeking to give advice or trying to fix things but by being humble and learning to listen and feel and allowing ourselves to be led by God's Spirit.

Fortunately, we do not have to look very far to discover the extent to which social realities will be shaped in God's new world. Besides the Scriptures already referenced, the book of Revelation gives us another vision for what this future reality might look like. Revelation 7 depicts a great multitude from every tribe, nation, and tongue worshiping the Lamb. The picture is a vivid one, with humanity (despite ethnic differences and language) uniting as one in worship of the Creator. While this vision does not align with what we see in the wider society, or in many communities of faith, it nevertheless becomes the end to which we are all oriented. God has set the created order on a certain trajectory to be transformed by the Son and Spirit, and Christians and communities of faith have the responsibility to work toward the renewal of the present world to reflect this coming kingdom. We believe that work in psychology can be an extension

29. Martin Luther King Jr., "Letter from Birmingham City Jail (1963)," in *Testament of Hope: The Essential Writings and Speeches*, ed. James Melvin Washington (New York: HarperCollins, 1986), 299.

of the work of the church in cultivating restorative spaces for those who have been stigmatized, marginalized, or oppressed.

The Incarnation of Christ as the Model for What It Means to Be Human

We've already noted how psychology alone cannot provide a comprehensive ontology that tells us everything about human nature. Yet psychology's methodological naturalism does not mean that Christians who practice psychology must also subscribe to a purely naturalistic portrait of human nature.[30] Psychology offers important insights into human personhood, but comprehensive statements regarding ontology (i.e., what it means to be human) are deepened and broadened when we consider the theological reality that God became human in Christ. This kind of theological broadening was evidenced by what we noted above regarding the proximate arenas of human existence that certain Christologies highlight, namely, that Christ's life and death move us to consider how we live and act toward others and how we work for justice and healing in the world around us—especially in our work within the discipline of psychology.

The reality of Christ taking on flesh is a core aspect of Christian theological anthropology and a Christian ontology of being. Although psychology speaks of the relational and social components of human personhood, the Christian theological tradition would suggest that psychology can speak of these realities and study these realities only because God has created humans as relational and social creatures. Furthermore, although psychology provides a helpful means for understanding the various relational and social aspects of humanity, psychological explorations are not always informed by Christian or theological conceptions of personhood. Christians who study psychology can use and greatly benefit from psychology's insights, and there are considerable areas of overlap, but our view of humanity is not informed only by psychology. For instance, God's affirmation of humanity in Christ and God's revelation of

---

30. Peter Hampson, "Theology and Psychology," in *Christianity and the Disciplines: The Transformation of the University*, ed. Oliver Crisp, Gavin D'Costa, Mervyn Davies, and Peter Hampson (London: Bloomsbury, 2014), 119–20.

God's own self through Christ both expands on and reorients the insights into humanity that are gleaned in and through psychology. Christ as the One who lived an abundant and flourishing life becomes the model—the exemplar—of a life lived fully and abundantly. It is Christ who is the epitome of what it truly means to be human, and it is Christ, as the paradigm of God's determination of the creature, who "actualizes human personhood rather than stunts the creature's freedom."[31]

We are discussing Christology and theological anthropology (i.e., what it means for humans to be created in the image of God) in the same chapter because we understand Christ to be the perfect embodiment of humanity. Much of the discussion about humanity in the integration literature has tended to focus on the *imago Dei* apart from a consideration of what it means for humanity to be re-created, renewed, and restored by Christ. In addition, as Dallas Willard has noted, popular church culture's message about morality and the sinful tendencies of human nature has resulted too often in a "gospel of sin management" rather than an emphasis on the freedom, wholeness, transformation, and restoration that new life in Christ brings.[32] Even within the psychology and theology literature, there is the tendency to focus almost exclusively on the depraved state of humanity.[33] As a result, those studying and teaching psychology are in need of a more holistic view that highlights humanity's wholeness and restoration—one that conceives of humanity as moving toward a particular telos. Rather than a static notion of humanity, a view of this kind emphasizes the dynamic, developmental processes by which humans are conformed into the image of Christ.[34]

---

31. Gunton, *Triune Creator*, 183. Or, in Wolfhart Pannenberg's terms, "our destiny . . . is brought to fulfillment by Jesus Christ." *Systematic Theology*, trans. G. W. Bromiley (Grand Rapids: Eerdmans, 1997), 2:210.

32. Dallas Willard, *The Divine Conspiracy: Rediscovering Our Hidden Life in God* (New York: HarperCollins, 1998), 35–39.

33. We owe this insightful analysis of the literature to David N. Entwistle and Stephen K. Moroney, "Integrative Perspectives on Human Flourishing: The *Imago Dei* and Positive Psychology," *Journal of Psychology and Theology* 39, no. 4 (2011): 295–303.

34. Lydia Kim-van Daalen, "The Holy Spirit, Common Grace, and Secular Psychotherapy," *Journal of Psychology and Theology* 40, no. 3 (2012): 229.

In light of the New Testament's witness of Christ being the image of God (2 Cor. 4:4; Col. 1:15), Christ plays a central role in our understanding of what it means to be human creatures likewise made in the *imago Dei* (Rom. 8:29; 1 Cor. 15:49). Even though the term itself comes from the passage in Genesis 1:26–27 where the creation story speaks of God creating humanity in God's image, the *imago Dei* takes on new meaning as the New Testament authors deploy it in order to understand the theological significance of the person and work of Christ. For example, the apostle Paul suggests in Colossians 1:15–23 that Christ illuminates true human person-hood and transformation. According to Paul, Christ remains the perfect example of the embodied Word, both creature and Creator, who is both fully human and fully divine.[35] Oliver Crisp notes that "human beings are made in the image of God by being made in the image of Christ."[36] Similarly, Karl Barth famously argued that the "ontological determination of humanity is grounded in the fact that one man among all others is the man Jesus."[37] In other words, Christ as the true image of God is the example for humanity because Christ reverses the pattern of fallen humanity, thus bringing about restoration and healing. This reversal of the human story by Christ, through the power of the Spirit, is a description of the re-creating and redirecting of true human destiny through Christ's life, death, and resurrection.[38] Humanity is created with the capacity to image God through Christ, both individually and collectively. In love, God allows those who might not acknowledge Christ or God to still experience aspects of thriving through God's common grace. Christians thrive through their participation in the life of the triune God and as they become more like Christ—and non-Christians also have the

---

35. Colin Gunton and Robert W. Jenson, "The *Logos Ensarkos* and Reason," in *Reason and the Reasons of Faith*, ed. Paul J. Griffiths and Reinhard Hütter (London: T&T Clark, 2005), 83.

36. Oliver D. Crisp, "A Christological Model of the *Imago Dei*," in *Ashgate Research Companion to Theological Anthropology* (Burlington, VT: Ashgate, 2015), 225.

37. Barth, *Church Dogmatics* III/2, 132.

38. Colin Gunton, *The Promise of Trinitarian Theology* (New York: T&T Clark, 1997), 186; Gunton, *Christ and Creation* (Milton Keynes, UK: Paternoster Press, 1992), 30.

capacity for relationship with God, though they may not exercise this capacity in the same way.[39]

Christian Anthropology in Dialogue with the Psychological Sciences

Both psychology and Christian anthropology are interested in the proximate features of human existence. Although ultimate realms of existence (i.e., eschatological hope and resurrected bodies—yes, bodies!) are essential features of Christian anthropology, the proximate realms of human existence are the key points of overlap between psychology and theology. For instance, from a Christian anthropological standpoint, it is the work of both the Son and Spirit within the material and embodied existence of human lives that brings persistent and consistent healing, whether social, emotional, mental, or behavioral. By focusing on these more proximate concerns, we are able to move from abstract theological reflections toward a consideration of more concrete matters such as the relational and social capacities of humanity, the embodied nature of the human creature, and the malleability and dynamism that occur in human development. While we are intentionally not including a lengthy survey of the various viewpoints of the image of God (because these can be found easily elsewhere), these three components of Christian anthropology are especially important for engaging in theologically informed psychology.

Relational and Social Capacities of Humanity

One of the chief points of connection between Christian conceptions of human personhood and psychology's understanding of humanity is how both disciplines describe the relational and social dimensions of human nature. In terms of Christian anthropology, the relational dimensions of how God created humanity are quite clear. Starting with the creation story in Genesis, God creates humanity within a network of relationships, and these relationships include

---

39. Jason McMartin, "The Theandric Union as *Imago Dei* and *Capax Dei*," in *Christology Ancient and Modern: Explorations in Constructive Theology*, ed. Oliver D. Crisp and Fred Sanders (Grand Rapids: Zondervan, 2013), 136–50.

God, other humans, nonhuman animals, the earth, and our own selves. Knowing that God's Spirit moves and works in all aspects of this relational matrix, we also understand that when any of these relationships is broken, misguided, or disjointed, we are not living the fullest life that we can live.

Echoing Scripture, psychology also operates with a fundamentally social and relational portrait of human nature—as well as recognition that relationships can make or break us. Children exposed to consistent abuse and trauma learn to be fearful about relationships and the world around them, whereas children who are lovingly nurtured develop a sense of confidence about themselves and can learn to explore the world from the secure base of their caregiver. Here we find evidence that Scripture's command to love God and love neighbors is not only instructive about how we should treat one another but also has the effect of strengthening relationships and social bonds over time. Christ came to bring a new order to our relational world, a relational reordering of priorities that properly situates us within the created realm and, in turn, enhances our capacity to flourish as the relational creatures we are.

Embodied Nature of the Human Creature

As theologians have attempted to discern from Scripture what makes human nature unique, a common critique is that their descriptions of the *imago Dei* often drift into abstractions that easily overlook or simply dismiss the significance of human embodiment. To avoid this common error, we must foreground and not forget the "earthy, embodied dimensions of humanness."[40] Theological explorations of human nature that focus only on intelligence or language to describe humanity are far too narrow and dismiss the vast complexities of how body, brain, mind, and spirit are intricately intertwined. The term "embodiment" is the word we use to speak of the whole-person view of humanity that comprises body, brain, mind, and spirit in a psychosomatic unity. We've already noted that being created in the image of God means that we are re-created in Christ's image and

---

40. J. Wentzel van Huyssteen, "Theology, Science, and Human Nature," *The Princeton Seminary Bulletin* 27, no. 3 (2006): 201.

we possess the capacity to relate to God and others, but the emphasis on embodiment here sums up the important fact that Christ had a body and that to be human is to exist in a certain embodied form that shapes our very nature. Moreover, as humans we cannot relate in any other way with God, others, and the world around us except through our own embodied selves.

On Being and Becoming Human

"Becoming" is simply the term we are using to describe the dynamic state of change that occurs in the physical, biological, and spiritual realms of human growth and development over time—from conception, infancy, and childhood on up to adulthood. From a theological perspective, authentic human identity is never something that is fully achieved or possessed by the human creature but is something that we more closely approximate as we grow and change over time. Becoming human is therefore a "perpetual movement of receiving and responding" to the gifts and the absolute generosity of the triune God.[41] Susan Ross similarly observes that being created in God's image is "not a static reality found in one discrete and identifiable part of ourselves" but is rather a "dynamic process of opening ourselves to the world, caring for it as best we can with all of our abilities, and reflecting on our place in the world with both awe and lament."[42] In other words, to conceive of humanity in terms of the *imago Dei* is to understand the human person as a fundamentally dynamic creature—with change and growth happening over time as humans live in reciprocal relationships with God, others, and the created realm.[43]

Every human person enjoys gifts from God and can flourish when they move toward relating to themselves and with others in ways that

41. John Webster, "The Human Person," in *The Cambridge Companion to Postmodern Theology*, ed. Kevin J. Vanhoozer (Cambridge: Cambridge University Press, 2003), 228.

42. Susan A. Ross, *Anthropology: Seeking Light and Beauty*, Engaging Theology: Catholic Perspectives (Collegeville, MN: Liturgical Press, 2012), 139.

43. For an elaboration on the dynamism of human personhood, see Jack Balswick, Pamela E. King, and Kevin Reimer, *The Reciprocating Self: Human Development in Theological Perspective* (Downers Grove, IL: IVP Academic, 2016).

reflect the compassionate and self-giving love of Christ. This element of flourishing is what we might consider the common telos of human being and becoming, and it is made possible by the wider work of the Spirit of God in the world; however, flourishing or abundant life for the Christian also has a particularized telos. This distinctly Christian, developmental vision of thriving freely acknowledges that, through the Spirit, Christ is at work in our lives, which moves us to consider both proximate and ultimate arenas of human existence. Although the image of God in humanity is given structure through Christ, the "Spirit . . . realizes a particular pattern of life on earth."[44] Thus, the relation between Christ and the Spirit in regard to anthropology looks like this: Christ *redeems* and *organizes* a pattern for human existence in the world, while the Spirit *particularizes* and *brings freedom* within the structures of the world.[45]

A Journey rather than a Destination

If the human sciences have taught us anything in the past thirty years, especially through discoveries in neuroscience and neuropsychology, it is how malleable human development is. While genetic makeup does dictate functional structures of one's personhood, it provides only a rough sketch, and the rest is formed through complex environmental interactions as humans relate with the world around them.[46] Humans are shaped and formed as they interact and make meaning of the world, and this includes both physical and spiritual realities. Although developmental psychology speaks to how our cognitive structures and physical abilities are shaped along with the physical world around us—especially as infants—we also note that we are shaped by ongoing human engagement with the being and activity of God. Such a conceptualization affirms the significance of the human person's relational capacities and embodied nature, but it also recognizes that these physical, embodied

44. Gunton, *Christ and Creation*, 101.
45. Gunton, *Christ and Creation*, 107.
46. Warren Brown and Brad D. Strawn, "Self-Organizing Personhood," in *The Ashgate Research Companion to Theological Anthropology* (New York: Routledge, 2015), 96–97.

capacities do not stand outside the purview of the ongoing activity of Christ's Spirit.

Given that the Spirit creates new energies as the sustainer and perfecter of life, we should not be surprised that there could be dynamism and change over time when conceptualizing human nature from a Christian theological anthropological perspective. Put differently, the process of being conformed to the image of the incarnate Christ who is the *imago Dei* reflects an end or telos to which we will never fully arrive in the present age. Additionally, human nature itself is fundamentally dynamic, developmental, and in process. Consequently, we can say with some confidence that to be human as Christ is human is not about arriving at some destination or disembodied state of being, but about embarking on a fully embodied journey toward the kind of abundant life that was made possible through the incarnation.

Questions for Reflection and Discussion

1. As a human, what does it mean to be a body rather than to have a body?
2. What messages about the body and emotions (implicit or explicit) did you receive from your religious tradition?
3. What might it look like to be Christ incarnate to those we serve through clinical and research psychology?
4. In light of the contributions of Black, feminist, and liberation theologies, what does a preferential option for the poor, oppressed, and marginalized mean for your studies and future work as a psychological practitioner?

Resources for Reading and Exploration

Balswick, Jack O., Pamela Ebstyne King, and Kevin S. Reimer. *The Reciprocating Self: Human Development in Theological Perspective*. 2nd ed. Downers Grove, IL: IVP Academic, 2016.

Brown, Warren S., and Brad D. Strawn. *The Physical Nature of Christian Life: Neuroscience, Psychology, and the Church*. Cambridge: Cambridge University Press, 2012.

Gutiérrez, Gustavo. *A Theology of Liberation: History, Politics, and Salvation*. Translated by Caridad Inda and John Eagleson. Maryknoll, NY: Orbis Books, 1988.

Thurman, Howard. *Jesus and the Disinherited*. Boston: Beacon, 1996.

PART 2

The Psychologist as Theologian

5

Research Psychology as Experimental Theology

Key takeaways from this chapter:

- We can know God more deeply in and through scientific exploration of the created order.
- Psychological science can be celebrated and critiqued from a theological perspective.
- Psychological research does not provide an exhaustive account of the human, but it does enable wisdom by helping us avoid error.
- Theology and psychology are not in conflict; they are complementary forms of knowing our world.

If I (Kutter) am being perfectly honest, I've always been a bit of a mystic. In fact, some of the most vivid memories from my childhood involve moments when I would lie on my back staring up at the summer sky, watching the gentle rustling of the leaves on the trees, awestruck by the sheer beauty and elegance of the world that surrounded me. In these moments, however sporadic and fleeting they may have been, the whole of the created order seemed to be saturated with a kind of energy that held all of its various parts together. Words are inadequate to describe these experiences, but Gerard Manley Hopkins comes close when he says that "the world is charged with the grandeur of God."[1] It was as if the rocks, the trees, the wind, and the sky were all conspiring together, calling me to know the natural world on a deeper level—to explore its many intricacies, to be ever more curious about its numerous eccentricities, to appreciate its infinite complexity.

Scripture is filled with similar descriptions of God speaking through the created order. Consider the following verses:

> The heavens declare the glory of God;
> the sky displays his handiwork. . . .
> Its voice echoes throughout the earth;
> its words carry to the distant horizon.
>
> Psalm 19:1, 4

> For since the creation of the world his invisible attributes—his eternal power and divine nature—have been clearly seen, because they are understood through what has been made.
>
> Romans 1:20

Just as the poetry of the psalmist and Paul's letter to the Romans suggest, one of the great mysteries of creation is that it is indeed capable of communicating information about God's glory and power and nature to us. But something more was taking place on those warm summer evenings when I was a child, something far more elemental. Charged as it was with God's grandeur, the material world was not simply speaking to me or delivering information to me but was inviting me into a deeper form of communion with the One whose Spirit makes reality itself a possibility.

In more ways than one, these early experiences of witnessing "the heavens declare the glory of God" (Ps. 19:1) have motivated most of my life's work, both theological and psychological. My fascination

---

1. Gerard Manley Hopkins, "God's Grandeur," in *Poems and Prose* (New York: Penguin Books, 1985), 27.

with the beauty of the created order motivated my studies in theological aesthetics, which has been the focus of most of my research, writing, and teaching as a theologian. At the same time, the undeniable elegance of the natural world compelled me to dabble for most of my life in the natural sciences and, eventually, to pursue a second PhD in psychological science. I love generating speculative theories about humanity's capacity to see and understand God's "invisible attributes" in and through the beauty of "what has been made" (Rom. 1:20), but the theology of creation we outlined in chapter 2 would also suggest that the material world itself harbors evidence of God's ongoing presence and activity. In fact, the apostle Paul goes one step further, claiming that the entirety of God's project in the world hinges on the empirical falsifiability of the bodily resurrection of Jesus as a concrete historical event. "If Christ has not been raised," says Paul, our faith is not only "useless," but "we should be pitied more than anyone" (1 Cor. 15:17, 19).

This is not to suggest that we can (or ever will) "prove" that the resurrection happened or that God exists through modern scientific means. Nor does it mean that the apostle or the psalmist shared the same concerns as contemporary people when they wrote about creation's capacity to disclose certain of God's attributes. These authors knew nothing of the scientific method or contemporary modes of empirical research. This is simply to say that people of Christian faith can and should approach scientific inquiry with a sense of enthusiasm and gusto, exploring both human and nonhuman creation with the confident expectation that, in doing so, they are developing a more robust and intimate understanding of their Creator. In this regard, the psychological sciences serve as a perfect example. By engaging in psychological research that explores the underlying dynamics of people's thoughts, emotions, and behaviors, we not only gain insight into what it means to be human but also come to a deeper understanding of the God in whose image human beings are made.

This chapter considers the theological significance of psychology as a research science, motivated by the prospect of knowing God more deeply by exploring what God has created. The reasons for this particular focus are twofold. The first is the simple fact that not everyone studying psychology will end up being a therapist. Nor should they! Experimental research is indispensable for the practice of psychology. It informs the various theoretical frameworks that clinicians adopt in their practices and provides evidence-based resources that enable therapists to determine the interventions best suited for the specific needs of their clients.

The second reason is that, from a historical perspective, contemporary psychological researchers come from a long line of women and men who pursued research science because they too wanted to know more about the amazing world we inhabit and, by doing so, to come to a deeper and more intimate understanding of the God who created it.[2] As a result, for centuries, scientists (psychological and otherwise) conceived of their life's work as fully commensurate with their Christian vocation. To engage in the production of knowledge as a psychological scientist was not a mere personal interest or even a profession; from a theological perspective, it was a calling. And we believe the same can be said for those conducting experimental research on the leading edge of psychological science today.

Thus, the primary goal of this chapter is to draw on the theological categories we have covered so far in order to understand more fully the ways in which the Christian faith might enable students of psychology to engage both critically and constructively in the task of psychological research. To do so, however, we need to first unmask a particularly pernicious narrative about the aims and origins of modern science that threatens to undermine this goal before we even begin.

On the Origins and Aims of Modern Science

A long-standing and fairly influential definition of theology can be found in the work of eleventh-century theologian Anselm of Canterbury, whose theological motto was "faith seeking understanding" (*fides quaerens intellectum*).[3] Anselm and other pre-Enlightenment

2. "From Copernicus through Galileo to Newton and beyond, most early modern investigators of nature's regularities understood themselves to be discovering the rationality with which God had imbued his creation." Brad S. Gregory, *The Unintended Reformation: How a Religious Revolution Secularized Society* (Cambridge, MA: Belknap Press, 2012), 379.

3. Anselm, *Proslogion* II, accessible at https://sourcebooks.fordham.edu/basis /anselm-proslogium.asp#CHAPTER%20I.

philosophers who embraced this turn of phrase were not suggesting that "faith" (i.e., what one believes based on nonreflective intuition or the testimony of others) could or should be replaced by "understanding" (i.e., what one believes based on reason), as if faith were a deficient or inferior form of knowledge. Rather, for Anselm, faith is the necessary precursor and precondition for any knowledge at all. There simply is no form of human reasoning or any other kind of psychological process that can be separated from our precritical faith commitments. Or, to borrow from Trevor Hart, a contemporary theologian whose work echoes this historic perspective, all human thought is "faith thinking."[4]

If the first thought that comes to your mind in response to Anselm's motto is that it might work perfectly fine for theology because theology is all about faith, but it does not apply to science because science is all about setting faith aside in order to pursue some kind of objective knowledge, you would not be alone. In fact, one of the more common narratives regarding modern scientific inquiry is that it is capable of delivering a detached, purely objective take on the world—what might be called "epistemological objectivity." In certain respects, this is not an entirely unfounded view. One of the main reasons that the gold standard of experimental design features randomized controlled conditions to which participants and researchers are all "blind" is because researchers want to remove the influence of human subjectivity from their studies as much as possible. But the scientific method itself forces us to acknowledge that, although the data this kind of research generates can be both credible and reliable (i.e., we have good reason to trust it), it is not "objective" in any absolute sense. In fact, the scientific method doesn't allow for any finding to go without qualification. The scientist merely accepts or rejects null hypotheses based on statistical probabilities and, in doing so, is always making provisional claims that are by definition never final and always open to falsification.[5]

4. Trevor Hart, *Faith Thinking: The Dynamics of Christian Theology* (Eugene, OR: Wipf & Stock, 2004).
5. "The court of science never passes a final judgment, but constantly re-evaluates the evidence to arrive at our current understanding. . . . The evidence will win out in the end. Science . . . is not perfect, but science is still our best bet for understanding

So the problem isn't science. The problem is that an overly simplified story regarding the historical relationship between the sciences and the Christian faith has created a series of artificial and often misleading distinctions between the various ways that humans come to know and understand their world (i.e., epistemology). For instance, a common assumption that is prevalent among scientists and laypersons alike is that faith and science constitute two mutually exclusive, even antithetical domains of knowledge, and, as such, have always been in conflict. Popularized over the course of the past few decades by scientists from various subdisciplines like Carl Sagan, Richard Dawkins, Sam Harris, and Daniel Dennett, and more recently by the likes of Neil deGrasse Tyson, this narrative suggests that modern science was birthed during the "dark ages," a time when religious institutions and leaders actively squelched any knowledge that might undermine their authority or threaten their grip on power. As the story goes, thanks to an intrepid group of scientists and freethinkers who were committed to pursuing the truth at any cost (e.g., accusations of heresy, excommunication, or even death), citizens of Western societies were eventually able to break free from the religious dogmatism that kept them in a state of oppression and servitude and enter a world illuminated only by the light of scientific truth. The conclusion that naturally follows from this historical narrative is that, as scientific knowledge advances, religion and its many trappings will one day disappear altogether, rendered obsolete by a much more sophisticated understanding of reality that has moved far beyond the naivete of our religious past.

The problem with this story is that it is at best incomplete and at worst misleading. As historian Brad Gregory has argued, not only were most of the first modern scientists in the West people of Christian faith who were exploring the natural order as created by God, but the great majority of the institutions that supported their expensive and painstaking efforts were church-sponsored universities, research societies, and religious orders committed to the promotion

---

the world around us and for improving our lives." Venki Ramakrishnan, as cited in Malcolm A. Jeeves and Thomas E. Ludwig, *Psychological Science and Christian Faith: Insights and Enrichments from Constructive Dialogue* (West Conshohocken, PA: Templeton Press, 2018), 49.

of knowledge about the material world.[6] It is also the case that, as psychological scientists Malcolm Jeeves and Thomas Ludwig have pointed out, the conflicts involving science and faith that have arisen over the past two millennia have been real and consequential, but they have been almost entirely conflicts between competing scientific paradigms (endorsed by Christians on both sides) or competing theological frameworks (endorsed by scientists on both sides) and not between science and faith.[7] A well-known but largely misunderstood example is the 1633 trial of Galileo, during which "his judges rightly considered themselves supported by the mainstream science of their age and the previous millenia. . . . Galileo's support came mainly from theologians and church leaders, including disciples of the Benedictine mathematician Benedetto Castelli, and . . . the archbishop of Sienna Ascanio Piccolomini."[8] In other words, Galileo's accusers—all of whom were Christians—rejected heliocentrism based on prevailing scientific accounts of the universe. In contrast, his supporters—all of whom were Christians—defended his claims based on an emerging scientific paradigm that was incompatible with geocentrism. Whatever antagonisms might have existed between science and Christianity during this episode and others like it, they were negligible compared to the enthusiastic embrace of science by Christians.[9]

There is some truth to the story, but it has little to do with the inevitable eclipse of religion by the sciences. Rather, the reality has more to do with the unintended consequences of the enthusiasm with which Christians embraced the sciences, coupled with the Protestant Reformations. As the Reformers sought to challenge a number of the abuses that were, in their mind, endemic to the hierarchical structures and ecclesial practices of the Roman Catholic Church, an

6. Gregory, *Unintended Reformation*, 379.
7. Jeeves and Ludwig, *Psychological Science and Christian Faith*, 34–35.
8. Jeeves and Ludwig, *Psychological Science and Christian Faith*, 26.
9. As Michael J. Buckley observes, "Many of the natural philosophers (as they were called at the time) believed that they could ground the apologetic argument better than the theologians. A good number of theologians seem to have concurred, and with that concurrence they signed on to the history that this dependence would effect." *Denying and Disclosing God: The Ambiguous Progress of Modern Atheism* (New Haven: Yale University Press, 2004), xiii.

open question arose regarding how church leaders and lay Christians could determine whose theological position was the most faithful. *Sola Scriptura* (Scripture alone) was a foundational doctrinal principle held by many of the Reformers, but in the absence of papal authority, to which authoritative sources might Christians appeal in order to know whose interpretation of Scripture was correct? In many cases, the natural sciences became the third-party arbiter of these theological disputes, in large part because they were perceived to be (1) objective, (2) based in natural laws that were universal in scope, and (3) essentially agnostic with respect to theological doctrine. Thus, in a somewhat counterintuitive move, rather than turning toward theological resources, Christians during the period of the Protestant Reformations drew on the natural sciences to support their theological claims precisely because they were not theological.[10]

As it turns out, though, when it comes to questions of theology, science gives with one hand while it takes with the other. The primary reason for this is because the governing assumptions of science that allow it to explain natural phenomena and produce ever greater knowledge of the natural world—epistemological objectivity, methodological naturalism, and functional atheism—serve as the very principles that disqualify religion or religious experience as legitimate objects of scientific inquiry, much less reliable or trustworthy sources of human knowledge.

As Gregory points out, the decision to turn to the natural sciences as the primary means for answering theological disputes produced a number of unintended consequences:

10. In his multivolume examination of the rise of modern atheism and its origins in domains that were equally religious and scientific, Buckley suggests the following:
> The lesson that emerges is that one cannot—in an effort to justify, found, or confirm assertions of the reality of God—bracket or excise religious evidence and religious consciousness and the interpersonal that marks authentic religious life and experience. . . . The most compelling witness to a personal God must itself be personal. To attempt something else as foundation or as substitute, as has been done so often in an effort to secure by inference the reality of God, is to move into a dialectical process generated by internal contradictions of which the ultimate resolution must be atheism. (*Denying and Disclosing God*, xv–xvi)

> Whether the natural world was God's creation or not, the [scientific] explanation of those regularities did not depend on theology or morality and was intellectually separable from them via amoral methodological naturalism. . . . Science enables human beings to do increasingly extraordinary things in manipulating the natural world but says nothing and can say nothing about what we should do or why we should do it. It is definitionally amoral. Yet power is overwhelmingly concentrated in the hands of political leaders and the wealthy, who are thus in a position to enact their moral preferences through the technological applications of science in disproportionately influential ways.[11]

The end result of this separation of science from faith is that the sciences are now in the midst of an identity crisis. The psychological sciences are not unique in this regard, but among the social and behavioral sciences, and even in comparison to some of the physical sciences, psychology continues to maintain a fairly rigid adherence to metaphysical naturalism as a discipline, almost to a fault. From a historical perspective, psychology emerged as a direct descendant of the Western intellectual tradition, which is indelibly Christian, and the modern scientific tradition, which was born from and animated by Christian commitments. Yet, given its dual commitment to the predictability of creation on the one hand, and the naturalist tradition on the other, there is now a question as to what this "science" is, how it functions in society, and how trustworthy and accurate its most basic moral, political, and legal claims are.[12]

We name these historical assumptions and this identity crisis not to suggest that the psychological sciences should be discounted or

---

11. Gregory, *Unintended Reformation*, 380.

12. Again, citing Gregory,

> Besides its countless contributions to human flourishing, the application of scientific findings has also contributed to untold destruction and human suffering, especially in the past century. Nor is this surprising, because science itself does not prescribe nor can it even suggest whether, how, or to what ends its findings should be applied. These are moral issues, about which the findings of science per se can say nothing. . . . The intellectual foundations of modernity are failing because its governing metaphysical assumptions in combination with the findings of the natural sciences offer no warrant for believing its most basic moral, political, and legal claims. (*Unintended Reformation*, 380–81)

disregarded as untrustworthy or fundamentally flawed. Instead, we name them so that we can critically reflect on them, opening them to critique and refinement by the broader intellectual community, which is what we now aim to do by drawing on the constructive theological categories we have developed in previous chapters. Because we will be building on the material we developed in chapters 2 and 3, some of the following will already be familiar to you. However, our focus here will be on the practical application of constructive theology for those engaged in the practice of psychological research.

A Constructive Critique of the Metaphysics of the Psychological Sciences

Constructive theology is neither indiscriminate celebration nor pure critique; rather, it's an exploration of both the benefits and drawbacks of every human endeavor. The psychological sciences serve as a perfect example. Governed as they are by the metaphysical assumptions of methodological naturalism, epistemological objectivity, and functional atheism, psychology presents the person of Christian faith with incredible tools for understanding human thoughts, emotions, and behaviors, but these are not uncomplicated tools. In order to use them well, students of psychology need to be able to recognize the limitations of the methods and tools of psychology, especially in those instances where theology might offer a substantive contribution to psychology's understanding of the human person and the world humans inhabit. As it concerns the metaphysical assumptions of the psychological sciences, the theological tradition provides people of Christian faith with resources for critiquing these assumptions and offering a constructive response when they are found wanting. Let us look at each of the assumptions we discussed in previous chapters as a way of demonstrating what a response of this sort might look like.

Methodological Naturalism

Recalling chapter 2, methodological naturalism implies a reduction of all that can possibly be known about reality down to observable material phenomena and nothing more. It is a view of the natural order as just that: nature. In other words, it is not the view of the Christian theological tradition, which has long claimed that the natural order is, in fact, created by a Creator. As such, creation is structured in a way that reflects the trinitarian God who made it, which is to say, as a dynamic, relational reality. To emphasize this distinction does not mean that one has to believe in a trinitarian Creator God in order to know anything about the world or human beings. However, a theology of creation does raise important questions about how those who operate within a naturalistic framework understand their obligation (if any) regarding the natural order of things. If the world and the humans in it are "nothing but" their materiality, then psychological scientists have no real obligation to relate to them in any particular way while doing empirical research.[13] But if both human beings and the nonhuman world are created, then all our endeavors—scientific or otherwise—are better understood as a response to that initial creative act. We are "respond-able" to creation; we are obligated to respond to the world as agents who are caught up in a web of deep relationality with both human and nonhuman creation. In and of itself, nature places no such obligations on us. Thus, a theology of creation expands on psychology's methodological naturalism, providing psychological scientists with the intellectual resources and philosophical rationale for why the humans they study are rightly understood not as objects of scientific inquiry, but as subjects to whom they are related and morally responsible.

Epistemological Objectivity

"Epistemology" is just a technical term for the branch of metaphysics concerning what can be known, and as we have said before, epistemological objectivity is the notion that science is capable of delivering objective knowledge about the world. But it is also both more and different than that. For many, the objectivity of scientific knowledge is thought to be superior to other forms of knowing, so

---

13. We owe the language of "nothing but" to Don MacKay, *The Clockwork Image: A Christian Perspective on Science* (Downers Grove, IL: InterVarsity, 1974), 72.

much so that it will one day be capable of providing an exhaustive explanation of each and every observable phenomena—a complete account of reality itself.[14] Importantly, though, exhaustive explanations of the world are simply a means to another end. Rather than merely knowing more about the natural order, scientific knowledge of this sort is ultimately aimed at mastering it. The assumption of epistemological objectivity, along with the privileging of this form of knowledge above all others, sets the stage for a vision of science that is both without any limits and self-evidently good.

But as philosophers of science from Thomas Kuhn to Nancey Murphy remind us, the knowledge science delivers is, in fact, limited, and in the absence of an appropriate level of humility before our data, science can (and in some cases does) cause a great deal of harm to the humans who wield it, especially in the hands of those who seek mastery over the natural order.[15] Of course, from a theological perspective, this stands to reason. God grants humans "dominion" over nonhuman creation in Genesis 1:28, but dominion does not mean domination, nor does it mean mastery or an unrestrained manipulation. Dominion here is better understood as a command for humans to harness creation's potential for the sake of its flourishing. In the passage that immediately follows, God places Adam and Eve in the garden and commands them to "care for" (*'abad*) and "maintain" (*shamar*) it (Gen. 2:15), further underscoring that, as creatures themselves, humans are not masters of the created order but stewards of

14. The era otherwise known as the Enlightenment ushered in a time in which data and empirical inquiry were elevated and, in many ways, absolutized as the only real instruments of knowledge. For a fuller picture of the Enlightenment's influence on scientific and theological knowledge, see Edward Farley, *The Fragility of Knowledge: Theological Education in the Church and University* (Minneapolis: Fortress, 1988). What is more, from the time the word "psychology" began to be used in the way it is used today, the people using it wanted to be engaged in science, not philosophy. In fact, as experimental science developed its capacity to explain the operations of the natural world through the scientific method, psychological scientists increasingly turned to empirical data as the only authoritative source for any kind of knowledge—psychological or otherwise. See Eric Shiraev, *A History of Psychology: A Global Perspective* (Los Angeles: Sage, 2011), 104–16.

15. For an excellent historical analysis of the modern naturalist tradition and its implications for science, see Nancey Murphy, *A Philosophy of the Christian Religion* (Louisville: Westminster John Knox, 2018).

it. Creation is not the territory on which humans exert their will to power but the garden they are tasked with cultivating.

For the student of psychology who is also a person of Christian faith, the notion of epistemological objectivity need not be abandoned, only reframed. The kinds of knowledge produced by scientific explorations are indeed reliably true. They are also potentially good, but only insofar as they are utilized in ways that lead to the flourishing of both human and nonhuman creation. From this view, it is neither possible nor preferable to master nature through the production of objective knowledge. What is more, when located within a larger theological framework, epistemic humility is not an impediment to scientific progress but serves as its necessary condition.

Functional Atheism

In certain respects, a functional atheism follows quite naturally from the methodological naturalism and epistemological objectivity that prevails within the sciences in general and the psychological sciences in particular. To be clear, there is nothing inherently wrong with nontheistic accounts of natural phenomena, psychological or otherwise. The issue is rather that, within the sciences in general and the psychological sciences in particular, atheism often functions as a totalizing narrative. It not only dictates what is and is not a legitimate object for scientific inquiry but also determines the explanations that scientists are free to entertain as they interpret the data they collect. If this were simply a reflection of the scientific community recognizing the limits of the scientific method and acknowledging that certain phenomena fall outside the bounds of empirical research, that would be one thing. But the real-world implications of this functional atheism are that the humans engaged in the production of scientific knowledge (i.e., scientists) tend to overreach in their estimation of what science can tell us about the world, and the science-consuming public often follows suit. Shorn of its theistic origins as an exploration of the created order, modern science is forced to bear a burden it was never meant to bear. Not only does it have to explain to us what it has discovered through rigorous experimentation but it is now also responsible for determining whether, how, and to what end those findings ought to be applied. The problem with this expectation is that science qua science is not equipped to function in this manner. It is a descriptive project, not a prescriptive one.

This was the very crisis that Nietzsche's madman recognized when he shouted for anyone who would listen, "God is dead! God remains dead! And we have killed him!"[16] It is important to note that Nietzsche's madman was not talking to Christians, and his proclamation was in no way exultant or celebratory. Instead, he was expressing a deep sense of anguish and disillusionment to his modern secular counterparts—to the women and men who thought that, given the clearly superior forms of knowledge provided by scientific progress, they could easily do away with silly superstitions like "God" and still somehow maintain the moral compass that God provided. Nietzsche is often disregarded by Christians given his explicit critiques of Christianity, but people of faith engaged in the psychological sciences would do well to keep the madman's warning in mind. To operate with the assumption that the sciences offer a total accounting of human life that can also provide us with answers to our deepest ethical dilemmas is a fool's errand.

Again, this is not to say that science is somehow bankrupt through and through, or that its deliverances are fundamentally suspect. If anything, it's quite the opposite. The sciences can and do provide us with reliable solutions for many of the problems that ail us and offer an unparalleled means for human flourishing. But on their own and in isolation, they are an incomplete and inadequate resource for directing our lives. Knowing this, Nietzsche suggested that we should all have the courage to take the functional atheism of the sciences to its logical end and move completely beyond any notion of "good" and "evil" that we have inherited from our morally oppressive religious traditions. That's one option. A Christian theology of creation, however, would suggest something a bit different—to reconceive of scientific explorations of the created order not as an atheistic or even agnostic enterprise but as a creative collaboration with the God who made it.

16. Friedrich Nietzsche, *The Gay Science (The Joyful Wisdom)*, trans. Thomas Common (Lawrence, KS: Neeland Media, 2009), 79.

Celebrating Psychological Science as Collaborative Cocreation

Now that we have outlined a few of the ways Christians might respond critically and constructively to the metaphysical assumptions of the psychological sciences, we can explore some of the ways people of faith might draw on a theology of creation in order to celebrate the contributions of the sciences. As we have discussed in previous chapters, science as a tradition assumes the knowability of creation, and it is also a tradition that can and does reveal God's presence. If we understand that what psychology and psychologists are doing has to do with the creative capacities humans are endowed with as stewards of God's creation, that should fundamentally change our approach to psychological science. Psychology is not "mere science" but is a creative capacity to shape creation and to steward and name aspects of creation. All the sciences are to some degree about classification and naming. But our naming of the world (and its phenomena) as psychologists creates a niche within that creative world with which we interact creatively. In turn, that niche re-creates us. Psychology is thus about collaborative cocreating. Let's consider three ways in which the psychological sciences might enable humans to engage in exactly this kind of collaborative cocreation.

Pursuing Evidence in a Post-truth World

One of the key ways psychological science provides a means for collaborative niche-making can be found in its pursuit of empirical evidence to ground its claims. Because the cognitive and perceptual capacities of the human creature are attuned to the structure of creation itself, we are able to know the world as intelligible (though complex). Although this is a deeply theological claim, it does not depend solely on theological commitments. Numerous evolutionary psychologists, many of whom explicitly reject any kind of theistic beliefs themselves, have noted the ways in which the architecture of the human mind has developed in order to navigate and respond creatively to our environment, including the emergence of a near universal capacity for belief in supernatural agents.[17] This of course does not mean that humans are equipped to know everything about their world. As the author of Ecclesiastes reminds us, the ultimate meaning of reality is something that will always elude us to some degree (Eccles. 3:11). It is, most fundamentally, a mystery. But mystery does not mean unknowability or irrationality; rather, mystery implies that there is too much to know. The created order is, in the final analysis, inexhaustible. And it is this very inexhaustibility that animates human creatures to explore their material surroundings through empirical means, pursuing an ever deeper but never complete understanding of the evidence they discover.

Indeed, if Paul's claims in Romans 1 about the knowledge of God that can be found in creation are true, then psychological scientists who are people of Christian faith should have no fears regarding what they might discover through their empirical research. But we can make an even stronger claim: if our theological understanding of human thought, feeling, and behavior is not in some way vulnerable to empirical data, then something is actually wrong. As we noted above, we always need to keep in mind the limits of scientific knowledge and the limits of human capacity to know (e.g., 1 Cor. 13:12), but for the Christian, empirical evidence doesn't just matter, it matters ultimately. To be sure, demonstrable evidence has always mattered in this way. Remember Paul's injunction to the church in Corinth: "If Christ has not been raised, then our preaching is futile and your faith is empty" (1 Cor. 15:14). But in a post-truth society in which "alternative facts" are entertained as true, and Christians are, statistically speaking, the subgroup in American society most skeptical of scientific findings, people of faith who are competent empirical

17. Indeed, a few of the more prominent psychologists engaged in this area of research are Paul Bloom, *Descartes' Baby: How Child Development Explains What Makes Us Human* (London: William Heinemann, 2004); Pascal Boyer, *Religion Explained: The Evolutionary Origins of Religious Thought* (New York: Basic Books, 2001); Justin L. Barrett, *Cognitive Science, Religion, and Theology: From Human Minds to Divine Minds* (West Conshohocken, PA: Templeton Press, 2011); and Jesse Bering, *The Belief Instinct: The Psychology of Souls, Destiny, and the Meaning of Life* (New York: Norton, 2012).

researchers are needed now more than ever.[18] In such a time as this, we can celebrate the scientific goals of objectivity and agnosticism in the face of empirical evidence as a means for drawing closer not just to "the facts" but ultimately to truth.

The Wisdom (and Folly) of Predictive Research

The history of psychology as a predictive science capable of influencing human behavior is riddled with cautionary tales. A prime example can be found in the work of a handful of psychologists in the behaviorist tradition who advocated for an approach to psychological interventions that verged on social engineering. For psychological scientists like David Hartley, J. S. Mill, and B. F. Skinner, human behavior could be explained (and predicted) in terms of the ways in which external stimuli condition people to respond through either positive or negative reinforcement.[19] Of course, behind this push to explain human thought and behavior in terms of empirically observable events was the assumption that the world generally and human society specifically were progressing. So proponents of empirical observation and analysis within the psychological sciences were not simply advocating for better methods of measurement, replication, and predictability. Theirs was a much grander vision than that. Experimental science was nothing less than the key to human progress—to the flourishing of the individual and the well-being of society as a whole.

In the wake of the various cataclysmic events of the twentieth century (e.g., two world wars, nuclear holocaust, eugenics), most of which were made possible by advances in modern science, these utopian hopes have proven to be misplaced. That being said, to understand human psychology from an empiricist standpoint is to acknowledge the incredible benefits of the predictive research sciences. Indeed,

18. For a recent study examining the links between American Christianity and science skepticism, see Elaine Howard Ecklund, Christopher P. Scheitle, Jared Peifer, and Daniel Bolger, "Examining Links between Religion, Evolution Views, and Climate Change Skepticism," *Environment and Behavior* 49, no. 9 (2017): 985–1006.

19. See, for example, B. F. Skinner, *The Behavior of Organisms* (Acton, MA: Copley, 1938); and Skinner, *Science and Human Behavior* (New York: Free Press, 1953).

what Augustine called "*scientia*" is the kind of knowledge produced through reasoned reflection—when one refuses to take a conclusion for granted or to accept a given theory uncritically.[20] It is an approach to knowledge that highlights the value of measurable data and analyses not because they are infallible but because they allow for public inquiry and debate from a community of learned researchers around a shared object of concern. It is also an approach that admits that reason and observation, while helpful tools, are themselves flawed and incomplete. In other words, in its purest form, the empiricism that has shaped the historical development of psychological science is less about proving with absolute certainty what is true than it is about the wisdom of avoiding predictable errors.

For instance, in the statistical hypothesis testing most commonly employed by psychological scientists, there are two kinds of errors: type 1 and type 2, which are more commonly known as false positives and false negatives. In terms of statistical probabilities, the only real way to decrease the chances of accepting something as true when it isn't, or rejecting something as false when it isn't, is to increase the size of the sample being studied. Even then, because there is always a chance that an experiment might be flawed or in need of further development, both the method and results of the experiment are made public so that others can attempt to replicate its findings.

To put this a bit differently, psychological scientists seek to decrease the odds of misunderstanding human thoughts, feelings, and behaviors by studying samples that are larger and more representative of the general population and then making their findings available to a wider community of scholars for correction and refinement. This approach has direct and immediate implications for both lay Christians and professional theologians who are often guilty of constructing theological theories based on a limited data set and without concern for the broader theological community. For instance, without denying the real significance of one's personal, subjective experience, much can go wrong theologically when definitive conclusions are drawn about God, humans, or the world in which we live based on a data

20. Augustine, *On the Trinity*, trans. Stephan McKenna in *The Fathers of the Church: A New Translation*, vol. 45 (Washington, DC: Catholic University of America Press, 1963).

set of one (i.e., my individual experience alone). In the absence of a larger sample size, the probability of making a type 1 or type 2 error is greatly increased. What is more, without a broader theological community—both historic and local—contributing to the analysis of these subjective experiences, individual interpretations are not held up to critique and correction, and thus are more prone to error.

The danger of committing these kinds of errors is only amplified in an age of (dis)information overload, especially when there seems to be equally legitimate anecdotal evidence for just about any and every theological theory. So, what is needed now is not necessarily more or better information, but rather *wisdom*—a mode of discernment that leads away from rather than toward predictable errors. The psychological sciences provide Christians with helpful tools that enable them to move in this direction with confidence, in no small part because the basic assumptions of predictive research align with a theology that would suggest the created order operates in ways that are, on the whole, stable over time and reliably coherent. Statistical inferences drawn from empirical data are by no means error free. Nor are they ideologically or theologically neutral. Still, in the absence of empirical support, wisdom is empty. Likewise, without wisdom, data is blind. Or, as Augustine might say, *sapientia* depends on *scientia*, and vice versa.

Thriving as Bridging the Nature-Niche Gap

As we discussed in chapter 4, the classical Western theological tradition has exerted a great deal of energy examining sinfulness and human depravity. Likewise, modern psychology, which also emerged from the Western intellectual tradition, has focused at times almost exclusively on the pathologies and maladaptive behaviors that inhibit mental health. In other words, the primary orientation for both fields of inquiry has been the healing of what is broken rather than the flourishing of what is whole. More recently, however, some psychological scientists have shifted the emphasis of their research from fixing what is broken to exploring how and under what conditions people thrive. In light of the theology of thriving we developed in chapter 4—one that reconceives of the *imago Dei* as a dynamic and ongoing process that moves the human beyond total depravity—we can celebrate these shifts as fully commensurate with God's larger project in the world.

For instance, in their most recent work, experimental psychologists Justin Barrett and Pamela Ebstyne King have suggested that because humans actively create the conditions to which later generations respond, one of the keys to thriving is to consider how our niche-making might generate environments that are more rather than less conducive to the "maturationally natural" cognitive capacities of human beings.[21] According to Barrett and King, by adjusting our niche-making in light of experimental research and the findings of evolutionary developmental psychology, we are able to bridge the gap that often exists between the structures of our mind and the structures of contemporary society, thereby promoting the flourishing of both human and nonhuman creation. In doing so, we are actively leveraging the contributions of the psychological sciences in order to collaborate with the Spirit of God in the world, cocreating niches that allow humans to thrive.

Sketching the Contours of an Experimental Theology

To recap, the biblical witness (e.g., Ps. 19; Rom. 1), the historic theological tradition (from Augustine to Anselm to Aquinas), and our own personal experience (as psychological scientists and laypersons) all suggest that something can be known about God in and through an exploration of the world God created. Thus, the claim we have developed in this chapter is that the human capacity to discern God's presence and activity in and through the things that God has made holds true for the sciences in general as well as the psychological sciences specifically. By engaging in psychological research that explores the underlying dynamics of people's thoughts, emotions, and behaviors, we not only gain insight into what it means to be human but also come to a deeper understanding of the God in whose image human beings are made.

Regardless of whether you personally resonated with (or even agreed with) every aspect of this chapter, if our basic description of

---

21. Justin L. Barrett, with Pamela Ebstyne King, *Thriving with Stone Age Minds: Evolutionary Psychology, Christian Faith, and the Quest for Human Flourishing* (Downers Grove, IL: IVP Academic, 2021), 26.

psychology as a research science has in any way affirmed your own emerging sense of calling as a student of psychology, then we will consider it a success. That being said, the reason our hopes for this chapter are modest is simply because not everyone is called to the task of experimental research—neither every person of Christian faith nor every psychologist. But for those who are, a few implications follow that we would all do well to consider.

First, no researcher and no research project is completely or absolutely objective. Importantly, this is not a theoretical or philosophical claim; it is, rather, concrete and empirical. The simple fact is that every form of inquiry is contextual. Not only does each research project have a horizon beyond which it cannot see but every researcher inhabits a particular social location that serves as the interpretive lens through which all data is filtered. What Hans-Georg Gadamer once called "prejudices" psychological scientists now call "content biases," which are the suite of cognitive processes with which every human being operates.[22] Content biases shape how researchers gather, analyze, and understand quantitative data. Every human being develops their cognitive capacities within a particular sociocultural location, which means these biases can operate implicitly, informing how researchers may unconsciously classify members of racially, sexually, and socioeconomically marginalized groups.[23] Every psychological scientist needs to be vigilant in naming and accounting for these biases, but Christians have an intensified obligation to do so given their theological understanding of humans and the world they inhabit as God's good-but-fallen creation. This does not mean that we can ever do away with our biases entirely. Again, there is no such

22. Gadamer explores the notion of prejudices and their role in human understanding in *Truth and Method* (New York: Continuum Books, 2004). It is somewhat anachronistic to suggest this is an equivalent concept to content biases, but the point is that, just like the term "prejudice," the word "bias" should not be understood in a negative or pejorative sense but rather in a purely descriptive sense. It is inescapable that humans interpret and understand the world through their own particular lenses and cannot do otherwise.

23. A helpful article elaborating on the dynamic interaction between cognitive biases and culturally learned implicit biases is Perry Hinton, "Implicit Stereotypes and the Predictive Brain: Cognition and Culture in 'Biased' Person Perception," *Palgrave Communications* 3 (2017), https://doi.org/10.1057/palcomms.2017.86.

thing as purely objective research. But it does call for a deeper and more pronounced commitment to cultural humility—a willingness to acknowledge all that we do not know and to recognize the limits of our research and of ourselves as researchers.

Second, when viewed from a theological perspective, the ultimate end of psychological science is justice (this will be discussed further in chap. 7). The first and potentially most critical step toward this goal is to identify and make explicit one's social location—that is, to reckon with our blind spots and account for them with wisdom and humility. But the psychological project as a whole cannot remain focused on the individual alone, or even the human alone. Rather, for psychological scientists to contribute to a more just and equitable society, a world marked by God's shalom, their research needs to address the broader systems and structures that create the conditions for injustice in the first place. Psychological research is not a passive description of phenomena but an active construction of the world we inhabit, which means that each of our research projects bears the potential for creating a niche that either prevents or enables the flourishing of its inhabitants. To be sure, this is a goal-oriented vision of psychological science, but it is not meant to suggest that experimental research could ever possibly fix all the injustices that plague society today. Rather, it's a way of imagining the task of psychology as contributing in its own unique way toward a much larger project, the consummation of which John envisions in Revelation as a newly created niche—one in which the tears, mourning, and pains of injustice will be no more because God will be fully and wholly with us (Rev. 21:4).

Third and finally, our exploration of the theological significance of the psychological sciences points toward what might be called an "experimental theology." We have defined this elsewhere as an approach to the Christian faith that "employs the research methods and psychometric instruments of the psychological sciences to construct theological theories capable of generating empirically testable hypotheses."[24] Some would reject this notion out of hand, based on the assumption that experimental theology is not actually doing theology, "for theology is

24. Kutter Callaway and Brad Strawn, "Experimental Theology: Theological Anthropology and the Psychological Sciences," *Journal of Psychology and Theology* 48, no. 1 (2020): 3–4.

not the kind of thing amenable to scientific experimentation."[25] But as we have hopefully demonstrated throughout this book, theology is a lived practice by which we pursue broader knowledge about God and a deeper, more intimate knowledge of God. If it is the case that we can come to know God in and through what God has made (Rom. 1:20; Ps. 19), and that faith is always a faith seeking understanding, then theology is not only amenable to scientific experimentation; it demands it.

Questions for Reflection and Discussion

1. What does it mean practically for the telos of psychological science to be justice? How does that change your approach to your own work in the field?

2. Where have you encountered tension with the metaphysical assumptions of the psychological sciences?

3. Other than creation, incarnation, and the doctrine of the Spirit, are there any other theological concepts that help you engage in psychological research?

4. Where do you see gaps between people and the niches they inhabit? How might your work in psychological science help bridge this gap?

Resources for Reading and Exploration

Barrett, Justin L., with Pamela Ebstyne King. *Thriving with Stone Age Minds: Evolutionary Psychology, Christian Faith, and the Quest for Human Flourishing*. Downers Grove, IL: IVP Academic, 2021.

Jeeves, Malcolm A, and Thomas E. Ludwig. *Psychological Science and Christian Faith: Insights and Enrichments from Constructive Dialogue*. West Conshohocken, PA: Templeton Press, 2018.

Murphy, Nancey. *A Philosophy of the Christian Religion*. Louisville: Westminster John Knox, 2018.

25. J. T. Turner, "On 'Experimental Theology,'" *Analytic Theology*, July 2, 2018, http://analytictheology.fuller.edu/on-experimental-theology.

6

Clinical Psychology as Practical Theology

Key takeaways from this chapter:

- Our emotional world is a vital way that God communicates with us.
- People are more than their diagnosis, and the labels a community uses to describe mental health disorders say as much about the community as they say about an individual.
- When Christian communities create authentic spaces where difference is embraced, those with mental health diagnoses are offered freedom from the oppression of stigmatization and are also included as full-fledged members of the body of Christ.
- As a collaboration with the Spirit of God, psychotherapy shines a light on unconscious patterns of behavior and attempts to lift them to conscious awareness so that persons may change.

I (William) remember the first time that I started going to a psychotherapist. I had moved to Los Angeles from Fort Worth, Texas, to start my PhD in theology at Fuller Seminary. I did what a lot of students do when they move to a new city; I rented an apartment and found a couple of part-time jobs that would help me pay for my books, rent, and some tuition. My jobs were working in a church as a part-time pastor and covering some shifts as a server at California Pizza Kitchen (I can still tell you what goes on their BBQ chicken pizza). Although I loved the people and the work I did with the church, I was frequently visited by a loneliness that can easily come to those who work and serve in ministry settings. I was starting to form some friendships, but between my doctoral studies and my job in the church, I had little time to be as social as I wanted. Being in a new city and just getting to know people, I was also unprepared for the emotional work it would take to do PhD coursework and serve in ministry. Over a short time, I began to feel a deep disconnect between my academic studies in theology (which I loved) and the actual place where people in my church were in their own spiritual journeys. The members of my church demonstrated an earnest and honest desire to follow God, alongside real-life struggles that any of us could have, like how to deal with family conflicts, drug or alcohol abuse/addiction, divorce, career discernment, and coping with depression or anxiety. My academic studies in theology had done very little to prepare me for these "real-life" issues, leaving me unsure how to support these church members as they dealt with all that life threw their way. To make things more difficult, I held beliefs about who I needed to be as a leader that put undue pressure on myself to always have the right answers and do things perfectly. I'll freely admit, I'm a recovering perfectionist. The combination of these elements often made me feel unable to help others or even to take care of myself. It wasn't long before I realized that simple answers to these questions did not exist, and I needed some help.

If you're not accustomed to asking for help, going to a therapist or counselor can be quite a humbling experience—or at least that is how I found it to be at first. It requires us to ask for help and to admit that we don't know everything. In other words, it puts us in a position of vulnerability. What I learned was that to even step through a therapist's office door is to take a risk, and it's a risk that requires courage. And just an aside, whether you're training to be a clinical psychologist or not, going to therapy yourself is something that you really must do.

As I progressed through therapy, what I found was a deep disconnection with parts of myself. I had neglected my own emotional states of sadness and loneliness for quite some time. In addition, I held some theological ideas about emotions and emotional states that made me believe that I didn't need to attend to these parts of myself. I realized that I had coped with these feelings of sadness or loneliness in a way that did more damage than good. Instead of acknowledging my emotions of sadness or loneliness, I would ignore or push down these parts of myself, press myself into my work (whether in studies or ministry), try to rationalize or think about my emotions instead of feeling them, push myself to do more, and then criticize myself when I didn't feel like I had done enough. Doing this over and over again throughout my adolescent and young adult years had made me a master at ignoring my feelings and emotions. But, as Brené Brown aptly talks about in her book *Daring Greatly*, it's impossible to numb certain emotions without numbing others.[1] When we numb or ignore sadness and loneliness, we also numb our experiences with joy.

In addition to this, the theology of my childhood had taught me that you couldn't rely on your feelings or emotions because feelings and emotional states could mislead you. Back then, my knowledge of God and my own spirituality was very much based on a rational faith that disregarded the body and emotions. It's not that faith doesn't have a component of reason, but much of my life I lived with a theology that didn't regard our bodies and emotions as significant, perhaps even central, to our spiritual lives. I had never even considered that God might be speaking to me through my emotional states, and I never considered until therapy that God was giving me important information about my own pain.

1. Brené Brown, *Daring Greatly: How the Courage to Be Vulnerable Transforms the Way We Live, Love, Parent, and Lead* (New York: Avery, 2012), 169.

Needless to say, therapy caught me off guard. My therapist, Rick, pointed out to me that God can be working in and under and through our emotional states. One of the first things I learned in therapy was that the ways we relate to ourselves can be ungodly and even cruel. Many times, these patterns of how we relate, treat, and speak to ourselves occur without us even realizing them. As I moved through my first year of therapy, I began to understand parts of myself better. What I found was that I was extremely afraid of being seen as inadequate and that I felt inadequate much of the time. My feelings of inadequacy made me feel like I had to do more. And yet when I did more, this kept me socially isolated and contributed to my feelings of sadness or loneliness. These insights alone were enough for me to begin to make changes, and when I asked what God would want to say to these sad and lonely parts of myself, I found that God wanted to speak to these places and bring wholeness to these aspects of my life. These parts of internal suffering were not absent from God's love and grace. I also learned, as Peter Scazzero discusses in *Emotionally Healthy Spirituality*, that our emotional world is a vital way that God communicates with us and is intimately connected with our spiritual life.[2]

Almost twenty years later, I'm still in therapy and continue to find it a valuable place where I grow and learn about God, others, my own relational world, and my own blind spots. I'm convinced that God doesn't want us to neglect these parts of our inner life and that God speaks to us through our emotions and our emotional world. There are many Christian churches, families, and communities that value the inner, contemplative, and emotional life. At the same time, there are many churches, families, and communities that do not—and instead operate with theological views of human personhood and emotions that cause harm. Much of the theology we have developed in chapters 1 through 5 is a corrective to some theological beliefs that discount the role of the emotions and the body, which is why, in this chapter, we aim to offer a constructive theological appraisal of clinical psychology from the perspective of one's Christian faith.

2. Pete Scazzero, *Emotionally Healthy Spirituality: It's Impossible to Be Spiritually Mature While Remaining Emotionally Immature* (Grand Rapids: Zondervan, 2017), 96.

Psychotherapy from the Perspective of Christian Faith

To understand psychotherapy from the perspective of Christian theology we must do two things. We must first deconstruct (or disintegrate) theologies found in certain church cultures that are damaging regarding mental health (like thinking that our spiritual life is disconnected from our physical bodies or that we should ignore emotional and bodily states that God also created). Second, we must deepen and broaden some of the existing Christian theological ideas that are found in Scripture but that are not regularly discussed in churches or integration classes in order to gain a fuller perspective of God's role in healing in a relational context like psychotherapy.

Deconstructing Theologies That Are Harmful to Mental Health Treatment

In a critique of Western mental health perspectives, Ethan Watters's book *Crazy Like Us* outlines how aspects of American psychology have brought "Western" conceptions of mental conditions and illnesses to other countries, much to the detriment of some cultures.[3] In one chapter, Watters focuses on anthropologist Juli McGruder, who traveled to Zanzibar to research schizophrenia. McGruder's research focused on the following question: Why do people diagnosed with schizophrenia in developing nations have a better prognosis over time than those living in industrialized nations? Working from an anthropological perspective, McGruder noticed that the relationship between the person with schizophrenia and their family was remarkably different than those in urban Western cultures. In a non-Western culture like Zanzibar, families were less reactive to the diagnosis, did not isolate the family member with schizophrenia, and had a narrative around the diagnosis (often a spiritual narrative) that created connection and empathy for the person with schizophrenia.[4]

From this research, Watters points out how relational and social connections can be lost through a label or diagnosis. More specifically, if a mental health diagnosis becomes the primary determinant

3. Ethan Watters, *Crazy Like Us: The Globalization of the American Psyche* (New York: Free Press, 2010).
4. Watters, *Crazy Like Us*, 127–86.

for how we relate to those with mental illness, then the relational and social connections that are vital to one's personhood are diminished. Watters's conclusion is that Western psychologists are trained to make a diagnosis, but the diagnosis keeps some from seeing and relating to a person in their entirety. The result is that the whole person is often missed by excessive focus on disease or mental illness. Because Western psychology has often operated from a "disease" model, the emphasis has been on what is wrong with a person instead of the things that are going right. These similar convictions were the impetus for Martin Seligman's turn toward what he called positive psychology, which emphasized what is going right with people, and studying qualities and virtues that contribute to positive health and positive mental health. Following Seligman, Mark McMinn has pointed out that positive psychology moves from a pathology model (where we simply focus on what is wrong) toward a health model (where we describe positive attributes of mental health). Positive psychology also asks what contributes to thriving and optimal development, positive coping strategies, and virtues that help people cope.[5]

We are also indebted to the work of Charles Taylor, who argues in *Sources of the Self* that individualistic and Western notions of the self and personhood have resulted in contemporary depersonalization and disengagement within wider society.[6] The intellectual trends that impacted theology, philosophy, and psychology were seventeenth- and eighteenth-century rationalist conceptions of humanity. From this view, not only are humans essentially minds, but it is only through our minds that we can discern the world, and the mind is of greater importance than bodily states and emotions. Historically, much of modern Western society (after the seventeenth century) has overlooked the personal and communal dimensions of human personhood. However, this Enlightenment trend is counteracted through a trinitarian framework that stresses the relational, social, and embodied dimensions of personhood. In keeping with the trinitarian approach to psychology presented earlier, we can acknowledge that

5. Mark McMinn, *The Science of Virtue: Why Positive Psychology Matters to the Church* (Grand Rapids: Brazos, 2017).

6. Charles Taylor, *Sources of the Self: The Making of Modern Identity* (New York: Cambridge University Press, 1989).

God's presence is wide and at work in the process of psychotherapy, just as God can also be in the field of medicine or research psychology or the arts.

It was American psychiatrist Karl Menninger (founder of the well-known Menninger Clinic) who noted that religion has been the "world's psychiatrist throughout the centuries."[7] All major world religions contain frameworks that impact a psychology of human personhood and offer visions for how healing should take place. Christianity is no different in this regard. In fact, Christian theology and Christian communities (in all their varied forms) contain an understanding of what it means to be human and what healing consists of. The Greek word "*psyche*" is often translated as "soul" in English translations of the New Testament, but it can also be translated "self" or "personality."[8] It is from psyche that we derive our terms "psychology" and "psychiatry." Even these connections between terms suggest an overlap in the common interests of the inner life of humanity that both Christianity and psychology share. Although the Christian understanding of healing will differ from all the ways psychology conceives of healing, Christian notions of what it means to be human and what it means for humans to experience healing will nonetheless be translated in terms of how a particular tradition or church community addresses mental illness and their views on psychotherapy. A Christian community's theologies of creation, humanity, salvation, and the body are key doctrines that will directly impact whether that church or community upholds the importance of mental health treatment.

Likewise, the various theories that operate within psychotherapy each take shape within a tradition of psychological inquiry, but theories of psychotherapy represent practical and applied methods of research psychology. More importantly, though, engaging in psychotherapy over time directly impacts our way of being in the world—that is, the way we relate to ourselves and others. In fact, the more we learn about attachment, neuroscience, and emotions,

7. Karl Menninger, *Man against Himself* (New York: Harcourt Brace Jovanovich, 1938), 393.
8. Joel Green, *Body, Soul, and Human Life: The Nature of Humanity in the Bible* (Grand Rapids: Baker Academic, 2008), 30.

the more we understand about the connection that exists between the brain and the mind, how our emotional states are foundational elements of constructing relational "maps" of ourselves and the world around us, and how these affective maps allow us to form secure attachments to others.[9]

Christianity throughout the centuries has a lot to say about ways of being in the world. However, the Protestant conservative Christian church in the United States (especially within the past century) has often reduced the Christian faith down to a simple decision to "follow Jesus" or a one-time cognitive affirmation of Jesus as Lord, instead of emphasizing a lifelong, developmental process of being shaped and formed by the Spirit of God. The result is a theology of salvation and healing that reduces redemption to a spiritual state that neglects the whole person.

Toward a Whole-Person Approach to Mental Health

Recall from our discussion in chapters 3 and 4 that God actively upholds the life of the human creature and the created realm and takes no pleasure in the death of even those who are wicked (Ezek. 18:23). God's love extends far beyond the bounds of only the "elect." It reaches out to the whole world, motivated by a desire that all people everywhere come to know greater wholeness and abundant life.[10] We are dependent on God for life, whether we recognize it or not. Job 34:14 informs us that God is intimately connected with sustaining our lives, and if God withdrew God's Spirit, then all of humanity would perish. God as the creator sustains this "very good" creation and speaks a continual "yes" to the human creature and the created realm.[11]

While psychotherapy is not a religion (though some forms of psychoanalytic societies can become religion-like), both clinical and

9. "The mind is a relational and embodied process that regulates the flow of energy and information." Daniel Siegel, *Mindsight: The New Science of Personal Transformation* (New York: Bantam Books, 2010), 52.

10. Pamela Ebstyne King and William B. Whitney, "What's the 'Positive' in Positive Psychology? Teleological Considerations Based on Creation and *Imago* Doctrines," *Journal of Psychology and Theology* 43, no. 1 (2015): 47–59.

11. Jürgen Moltmann, *God in Creation: A New Theology of Creation and the Spirit of God*, trans. Margaret Kohl (Minneapolis: Fortress, 1985), 209.

developmental psychology do a good job of acknowledging the life-long process of being shaped and formed in and through our relationships. In this regard, Christian spirituality and certain forms of psychotherapy often overlap because of their shared interest in bringing healing to the human predicament.[12] Indeed, God's Spirit can work through folks like psychotherapists to bring about healing in large part because the (trans)formation of persons happens—or doesn't happen—through the ways that our personal relationships are ordered. This transformation occurs as God's Spirit is actively involved in every domain of our lives, so while we acknowledge that psychotherapy does not bring salvation, it nevertheless can be viewed as a relational process that God can and does use to bring restoration to people's lives. As a consequence, Christians who work as clinical psychologists are doing their part to shape and form their particular niche within the created order, partnering with the Spirit to direct humans toward wholeness.

Dimensions of Relationality

As mentioned previously, a trinitarian understanding of God emphasizes the relational components among God, humanity, and the world (chaps. 1 and 2). This interdependent, reciprocal notion of God's relationality offers a helpful corrective to aspects of individualism and depersonalization found in some Western philosophies and psychologies. More specifically, the five relational dimensions of human life (discussed briefly in chap. 4) highlight Christian theology's emphasis on the social, communal, and relational elements of how God made us, which helps inform our conception of psychotherapy. As humans, we stand in relationship with (1) God, (2) other humans, (3) our own selves, (4) other nonhuman animals, and (5) the earth. As we look at psychotherapy through the eyes of Christian faith, we note that God's Spirit moves and works in every aspect of this relational matrix, and we also understand that when any of these relationships are broken, misguided, or disjointed, we are not living the fullest life

12. David G. Benner, *Care of Souls: Revisioning Christian Nurture and Counsel* (Grand Rapids: Baker, 1998), 69.

that we can live. Psychotherapy focuses on many of these relational dimensions in order to bring about healing. Thus, from a Christian theological perspective, we can see how clinical psychologists are able to help patients have a fundamentally different kind of relationship with their own "self" and with others, thereby moving them in the direction of wholeness.

Nevertheless, in some Christian communities, knowledge of "self" or self-reflection can be seen as a selfish activity, which causes certain Christian communities to teach instead that one's focus should only be outward, on the needs of others. Yet, the Christian theological tradition has a strong precedent for self-reflection as a way to know God and better understand God's Spirit working in our lives. Our theological forebears recognized that to be human means that we have some degree of relationship with our own selves. As John Calvin noted, there is a reciprocal relationship between knowledge of God and knowledge of ourselves.[13] And as we see in Scripture, there is already a degree of respect and care for one's own self that is assumed in the command to love our neighbor as ourselves (Matt. 22:39). In short, the command to love our neighbor assumes that we have some degree of healthy awareness of and respect for our own selves.

That being said, self-awareness and respect for one's self are not the same as selfishness. Self-awareness requires us to live in an appropriate degree of gratitude to God for the life and gifts that have been given to us, along with a recognition of our limits as finite creatures created by an infinite God. For example, theologian Anthony Hoekema reminds us that one's self-image can be "either inordinately high (in the form of sinful pride) or excessively low (in the form of feelings of shame or worthlessness)."[14] And we know from our studies in psychology that either extreme in how we view ourselves (an excessive obsession with self or a disbelief in any self-worth) can be problematic. As we think about sanctification and transformation by

13. Calvin famously said, "Nearly all the wisdom we possess, that is to say, true and sound wisdom, consists of two parts: the knowledge of God and of ourselves. But, while joined by many bonds, which one precedes and which brings forth the other is not easy to discern." *Institutes of the Christian Religion*, ed. John T. McNeill, trans. Ford Lewis Battles (Philadelphia: Westminster, 1960), 35.

14. Anthony Hoekema, *Created in God's Image* (Grand Rapids: Eerdmans, 1994), 105.

the Spirit, we must at some level begin to believe and experience that we are valued and loved by God. And before we can treat others in a different way, we sometimes need to relate to our own self in a way that is commensurate with the reality that there is no condemnation in Christ Jesus (Rom. 8:1). Indeed, for students studying psychology, one of the most important (and difficult) lessons to learn is that God's Spirit also works to restore the relationship that we have with our own self.

Many of the clients that come from a faith background with whom I (William) work in psychotherapy believe that God loves them and that they are valued. But the way they criticize themselves can many times be quite harmful. Often these critical and violent ways of treating ourselves become most evident when we are in pain, embarrassed, or feel shame that comes from the voices of parents, siblings, caregivers, church leaders, or even our younger selves that we have internalized. Psychotherapy can be a place where we begin to develop healthy forms of self-awareness and self-respect. To be clear, when we talk about self-awareness, we are speaking about directing our attention so that we can engage in sustained reflection on our thoughts, feelings, and actions that we have toward ourselves. When we increase our capacity to reflect on these thoughts, feelings, and actions, we also develop a greater ability to reflect on our actions toward others and may better discern what God might want to say to us in this process. Because the five relational dimensions of human life are the very realms that God restores, it makes sense that one of the ways these realms can be restored is through a relational process like psychotherapy.

Incarnation and the Work of the Spirit through Psychotherapy

God is a relational God and has created humans as relational beings. We exist fundamentally in relationship whether we acknowledge this or not, and God interacts in the world through God's "two hands," the Son and Spirit.[15] Two key Christian theological themes

15. Colin E. Gunton, *The Triune Creator: A Historical and Systematic Study* (Grand Rapids: Eerdmans, 1988), 62.

that inform the work of psychotherapy that we will now highlight are the doctrine of the incarnation and the doctrine of the Holy Spirit (pneumatology). Both of these doctrinal themes help to conceptualize how we might understand God working in the process of psychotherapy, how God might use the uniquely personal encounter that psychotherapy provides, and how, for Christian psychologists, psychotherapy can embody the four key biblical themes of restoration, healing, justice, and love.

The Incarnation of the Son

In recalling what we established in chapter 4, we remember that God's incarnation sets the precedent for us entering the world of another person. The incarnation is about God's embodied presence, and the power of the gospel is rooted in how God took on flesh as a human person in Jesus Christ. Wholeness and healing can be aided through psychotherapy, and restoration occurs as God's Spirit works in the lives of individual people, with the additional acknowledgment that God also works through other people to bring healing and restoration. We talked previously about how shalom is the way God intended things to be, where God's justice and peace reign supreme, where relationships are rightly ordered toward love instead of toward greed, hate, or violence, and where the oppressed are set free. While God could have brought restoration to creation and persons in another way, God chose to bring restoration and healing in a very material and bodily way in Jesus Christ.

As David Kelsey has noted, being made in the image of God means we "image the image of Christ" and do things like Christ does.[16] Part of that imaging is to be in the world in a way that Jesus was by bringing about restoration and healing. Here we must remember that psychotherapists often act as an embodied (and incarnated) form of love for their clients or patients. Simply taking the time to sit with another human being and turn toward them with love and respect helps create a hospitable space in which people can flourish and healing can occur. Christ's work of salvation is an affirmation that Christ

16. David H. Kelsey, *Eccentric Existence: A Theological Anthropology* (Louisville: Westminster John Knox, 2009), 2:1027.

came to restore and redeem *all aspects* of human existence, and this includes our bodily, spiritual, and emotional lives. Viewed from this perspective, psychotherapy can be understood as one of the places where God's Spirit can move to bring restoration to the emotional realms of our existence.

The promise of presence, specifically God's presence, is one of the most powerful themes that runs throughout Scripture. God's presence is a consistent theme in the Hebrew Scriptures as God promises through a covenant to be present with Abraham and Isaac (Gen. 15:17; 26:24). When Moses and the Israelites doubted or were afraid as they made the journey out of Egypt and into the promised land, the reminder was that God would be present with them (Exod. 3:12; 33:14; Lev. 26:12). And the frequent message that God gave to the children of Israel through the prophet Isaiah and the prophet Jeremiah was "Do not be afraid," followed by the promise "for I am with you" (Isa. 43:5; see also Jer. 1:8; 42:11).

When we look at the New Testament, we find that these are also the bookends presented in the Gospel of Matthew. "God with us" is the meaning of "Emmanuel" in Matthew 1:18. We find the promise again when Jesus commits to be present any time two or three are gathered in his name (18:20). And we find it yet again in the last statement of Matthew's Gospel where Jesus promises to be with his followers even to the end of the age (28:20). In our pain, in our suffering, in our fear, the message of Scripture is clear: God does not abandon us or forsake us but remains with us, guides us, and suffers with us. We find that Scripture is also clear about the difficulties and suffering that we will encounter in this life, but it is in and through these difficulties—not in spite of them—that God promises never to leave or forsake us (Deut. 31:6; Heb. 13:5). God became incarnate in Jesus (John 1), and the Gospels are a testimony to the embodiment of God's love, power, and presence in the person of Jesus.

The promise of God's presence might raise a question though. How exactly is God with us today? As Christians, we believe that the Spirit of Jesus is with us all the time, whether we recognize it or not. Richard Rohr helpfully reminds us that we are already in the presence of God, and what is often absent is our awareness of God's presence.[17] God is working in our lives whether we acknowledge God's presence or not. And while God is with us through the Spirit, what we also find is that God frequently gives us embodied reminders of God's presence through people who actually "incarnate" the love and mercy of God to us. Most often we think of these people as pastors, priests, youth leaders, or mentors. However, it is also the case that clinical psychologists can perform a similar function, especially through certain practices like psychotherapy, where there is an emphasis on relational healing through virtues like justice, love, hope, and grace (which will be discussed in our next chapter).

In short, God can become more real to us through the process of psychotherapy because God is working through a psychotherapist who is the embodiment and incarnation of love, justice, peace, and mercy. On the other hand, any time a psychotherapist (or church minister!) does not practice love, justice, peace, and mercy in their relationships with others, damage can be done. Just as God promises to be present with us, we are often reminded of God's presence and power in our lives through healing relationships that incarnate God for us in real and tangible ways, and psychotherapy is one of those places where the Spirit of God can and does work to bring restoration.

The Pervasive Presence of the Spirit

To be clear, in no way are we arguing for psychotherapy as a substitute for the work of salvation, nor are we suggesting that psychotherapy fulfills the purpose and function of mission in the way that church does. Moreover, we are not holding up psychotherapy as an alternative or replacement for the embodied formation (and transformation) that occurs within the community of faith. What we are arguing is that, viewed from a theological lens and given what we established in chapter 3 regarding God's wider presence, psychotherapy can be used by God's Spirit to bring about restoration and healing as God works in the lives of both the psychologist and the patient. Although psychotherapy does not function in the same ways that

17. Richard Rohr, *Everything Belongs: The Gift of Contemplative Prayer* (New York: Crossroad, 1999), 28.

discipleship does in the context of Christian community, the work that is done in therapy can be spiritually nurturing and transformative. Given that many forms of popular church culture in the United States conceive of spiritual growth and transformation as occurring only within the walls of the church, it is important to recognize the broad and wide dimensions of God's presence and power through the Spirit, which necessarily includes the realm of psychotherapy.

To practice or pursue psychotherapy is therefore to participate in the ongoing work of the Spirit, whose movements are always inclined toward justice, peace, restoration, and freedom for the oppressed. Here we recall Luke 4:18–19, which we first mentioned in chapter 4. In this passage, Jesus is moved by the Spirit to proclaim good news to the poor, release for captives, recovery of sight for the blind, and freedom for the oppressed. One way to interpret what Jesus means by release from oppression in the Gospel of Luke is "freedom from both diabolic and social restrictions."[18] In the New Testament era, widows, orphans, the physically disabled, the poor, and prisoners were the common victims of marginalization. In contemporary society, many of these same groups are still marginalized, but we need to expand the list to include Black persons, Indigenous persons, persons of color, those suffering with mental illness, and the homeless. This list is by no means exhaustive, but people in each of these groups have experienced a history of oppression by cultural and systemic forces in the United States, and they continue to suffer from what can only be described as "diabolical social restrictions." The good news that Jesus proclaimed is that the work of the Spirit is to bring freedom from this kind of oppression and to move those who were once "outside" and living on the margins to being those who are now on the "inside." It is the great reversal that takes place in the kingdom of God. The outsiders are now welcomed as being valued and loved. The disenfranchised are welcomed to the table to eat with Jesus. We find very clearly that power, wealth, and privilege are not the scales that are used by God to weigh the value and worth of a human life.

18. Joel B. Green, *The Gospel of Luke*, The New International Commentary on the New Testament (Grand Rapids: Eerdmans, 1997), 212.

In terms of what this looks like in psychotherapy, the practice of creating space for others (and those whom we might perceive as different from ourselves) is indicative of the Spirit's work in the world. Even more specifically, the creation of space for those who have mental illness is one of the ways psychotherapy can be seen as a movement of the Spirit who works through human action to create a life-giving space for others. It is important to note that it is the Spirit's activity that enables humans to participate in this divine project by creating certain spaces (like the church) that are hospitable for human life.[19] In this way, the spiritual life of Christian communities creates "authentic human reality in the here and now" and allows persons to see beauty and dignity in those who might be different from themselves.[20] Empowered by the Spirit, humans are able to move toward more authentic living with themselves, others, and God.[21] But the Spirit also works to create unity amidst diversity—enabling persons and communities to engage in relationships with others in and through their differences. And when this occurs, those with mental health diagnoses are offered freedom from the oppression of stigmatization and are also included in the body of Christ: the church.

Toward a Theology of Clinical Psychology

From a Christian perspective, the work of psychotherapy can be framed within the justice narrative of Scripture. We are called to participate in the same kind of work that Jesus did for those who are oppressed. We can definitively say that the majority of folks who seek treatment through therapy are encountering some degree of emotional and psychological suffering and pain. Seen in this way, psychotherapy can be a place to move beyond a narrative about what is primarily "wrong" with persons (and labeling them with a mental

19. Colin E. Gunton, *Enlightenment and Alienation: An Essay Towards a Trinitarian Theology* (Eugene, OR: Wipf & Stock, 2006), 103.
20. Gunton, *Enlightenment and Alienation*, 103.
21. Froma Walsh holds that "the very essence of the therapeutic relationship and meaningful change is ultimately spiritual in nature, fostering personal transformation, wholeness, and relational connection with others." *Spiritual Resources in Family Therapy* (New York: Guilford, 1999), 3–4.

health diagnosis) and instead create a hospitable space for persons to talk about their experiences with mental health. Moreover, psychotherapy, from a Christian perspective, enables us to see beyond a diagnosis and grant people the dignity and worth that is endowed by their Creator. Richard Butman and Mark Yarhouse note that even in the midst of "incredible brokenness, it does not lessen the worth or dignity of each person we encounter. Practically speaking, this could mean that we have something to learn from each person in every encounter—if only because they bear the image and likeness of God."[22] Similarly, Scottish theologian and mental health nurse John Swinton reminds us that we need to see persons with mental illness as created and vivified by the Spirit of God, persons whose unique mental health experiences hold meaning.[23] And when located in a theological framework of common grace, it becomes clear that clinicians who function as mental health providers have been graciously given gifts to care for those who are often overlooked in our society. These gifts of God's common grace do not bring salvation, but they are graciously bestowed on people so that God's goodness may shine forth. They provide a foretaste of shalom—a glimpse of God's coming kingdom where persons are whole human beings.[24]

Consequently, Christians may understand their work in psychotherapy as participating with God in redeeming patterns of human thought and behavior by helping folks understand how they relate to themselves, others, and the world around them. Or to use the language introduced in chapter 4, the work of psychotherapy can help persons *discover* new things about themselves and *develop* these patterns in a direction that is pro-social or adaptive. In many cases, the relational patterns that we are unaware of are often the patterns that cause the greatest difficulties in our relationships. With this in mind, we might understand the work of therapy as helping patients

22. Richard E. Butman and Mark Yarhouse, "Psychopathology through the Eyes of Faith: Integrative Reflections for the Classroom and Beyond," *Journal of Psychology and Theology* 42, no. 2 (2014): 213.

23. John Swinton, "Time, Hospitality, and Belonging: Towards a Practical Theology of Mental Health," *Word & World* 35, no. 2 (2015): 171–81.

24. William Whitney, "Beginnings: Why the Doctrine of Creation Matters for the Integration of Psychology and Christianity," *Journal of Psychology and Theology* 48, no. 1 (2020): 44–65.

to discover how patterns of the past cause one to act in certain ways (often unknowingly) in their relationships and even toward one's own self.

According to Warren Brown and Brad Strawn, Jesus "made it clear that embodied and socially embedded ministry in a physical world is at the heart of the Gospel."[25] Given the embodied nature of the gospel, we can also see how change and transformation have an inherent *social* aspect.[26] And in fact, this movement toward a fully embodied, psychosocial wholeness is something that can begin in the proximate areas of existence between the clinician and client. Indeed, we can trust that the Spirit of God is at work in these spaces, leading those who are children of God (Rom. 8:9–10, 14) as they commit their clinical work to Christ.

If clinical psychology is a discipline that participates in the work of God in redeeming patterns of human behavior by helping people understand how they relate to themselves and others, then sin can be understood as something that we consciously choose to do; however, it can also include unconscious, destructive patterns of relating to others or to one's own self. Negative patterns of relating can't always simply be seen as conscious decisions to sin, since destructive ways of relating to ourselves and others are the result of us being sinful *and* the result of us being sinned against. Many of the internalized ways that we talk to ourselves we have inherited from our parents or caregivers. How many of us as parents have caught ourselves saying or doing something that our parents did, something that we vowed never to do? Or how many of us have found that the ways we deal with pain, anger, or sadness are similar to our caregivers' or parents' patterns of behavior? If the voices that we have internalized have been critical, hateful, or destructive, then often the ways that we deal with ourselves and others are shaped by those internalized voices of criticism or hatefulness. While Christian theology provides a broad

---

25. Warren S. Brown and Brad D. Strawn, *The Physical Nature of Christian Life: Neuroscience, Psychology, and the Church* (New York: Cambridge University Press, 2012), 168.

26. Steven J. Sandage and Jeannine K. Brown, *Relational Integration of Psychology and Christian Theology: Theory, Research, and Practice* (New York: Routledge, 2018), 11.

framework for understanding humans as malleable and shaped by social and environmental factors (1 Cor. 15:33), psychotherapy can help illuminate behavioral patterns that we (often unknowingly) act out within our relationships.

Mark McMinn similarly observes that the work of psychotherapists is to help patients "discover previously unexplored areas of their lives" by "peeling back the defensive cover of life and exploring the parts of life that are rarely considered."[27] In parallel to McMinn, we have argued that Christ's Spirit works to bring wholeness to the psychological and emotional aspects of our person, and this wholeness occurs within the created, material, and proximate realm of human existence (not only in a spiritual realm or the eschaton). Growth and change happen best, both behaviorally and spiritually, in healing relationships, and these forms of transformation are possible not only within the church but also through other practices—like psychotherapy. Healing relationships help us change by connecting us with someone supportive, kind, and loving—someone who has our interests in mind.

Clinical psychology's understanding of human behavior provides clarity regarding certain aspects of why humans act the way they do. In addition, it helps clarify the underlying conditions and motivations for both positive and negative behavioral patterns. Through psychotherapy, one's negative behavioral coping styles can be discovered, and, amazingly, God has made us with the capacity to recognize insights about ourselves that we did not know before. Once relational patterns are discovered, both the psychotherapist and the patient can work to develop these patterns of behavior toward wholeness, with the recognition that negative patterns of relating are usually rooted in real pain or hurt from the past. Christian Scripture outlines how all humanity is caught up in behavioral patterns that are sinful and how each person embodies practices that are harmful to others and one's self (whether we recognize it or not, e.g., Rom. 7).

We are consciously aware of some of these destructive behavioral patterns, but others occur without us knowing about them. Sometimes

---

27. Mark R. McMinn, *Sin and Grace in Christian Counseling: An Integrative Paradigm* (Downers Grove, IL: IVP Academic, 2008), 50.

we do consciously choose to relate in negative ways with other humans, but many times we relate wrongly because of ways that we have been sinned against. In doing so, we act out of our own woundedness. Illumination in both of these areas is necessary. While some people are actively aware of their harmful behaviors, there are also patterns that remain outside of conscious awareness. Broadly speaking, psychotherapy shines a light on unconscious patterns of behavior and attempts to lift them to conscious awareness so that persons may change.

Psychologists Robert Stolorow, Bernard Brandchaft, and George Atwood outline aspects of these unconscious processes through what they call the "prereflective unconscious."[28] While there are different aspects of the unconscious, the prereflective unconscious does not normally enter our self-awareness, forged as it is during early development through affective engagement with primary caregivers.[29] Patterns of behavior that form the prereflective unconscious, according to Stolorow, can move into conscious awareness through the sustained empathic inquiry of another. These elements of the prereflective unconscious emerge in the subjective space (the transference) between two persons.[30] In other words, as Paul Ricoeur has also suggested, social relations mediate self-awareness and self-consciousness.[31]

For example, while we all experience and feel the emotion of anger, the way we negatively cope with anger differs from person to person. Terry Hargrave and Franz Pfitzer describe several coping mechanisms: some withdraw; some blame others; some shame others or themselves through criticism; some may avoid responsibility or escape through emotional cutoff, alcohol, or drug use; or some may become violent or have outbursts of rage.[32] Generally speaking, how we negatively cope

28. Robert D. Stolorow, Bernard Brandchaft, and George E. Atwood, *Psychoanalytic Treatment: An Intersubjective Approach*, Psychoanalytic Inquiry (New York: Routledge, 2004), 7.

29. George E. Atwood and Robert D. Stolorow, *Structures of Subjectivity: Explorations in Psychoanalytic Phenomenology and Contextualism* (New York: Routledge, 2014), 102.

30. Atwood and Stolorow, *Structures of Subjectivity*, 6.

31. Paul Ricoeur, *Oneself as Another* (Chicago: University of Chicago Press, 1992), 326.

32. Terry D. Hargrave and Franz Pfitzer, *Restoration Therapy: Understanding and Guiding Healing in Marriage and Family Therapy* (New York: Routledge, 2011).

with anger constitutes a relational pattern in which we usually become "stuck" because it is part of our prereflective unconscious. Stolorow characterizes these patterns as "unconscious organizing principles."[33] Importantly, it is not that we are overwhelmed with too many ways to cope with anger (or too many organizing principles to help us think about anger); in reality, most of us have too few coping mechanisms.

Common grace allows us to understand that, even at the level of the prereflective unconscious, there are elements of truth that are worth discovering within the cognitions, behaviors, and emotions of human persons. It is therefore possible to see the work of psychology, and more specifically the practice of clinical psychology, as finding and developing these areas of truth that people possess and helping them understand their own patterns of behavior. We can discover truths about creation because God has fashioned a world that will disclose its secrets to those who inquire. Moreover, the Christian experience is informed by the basic belief that the Spirit of God works to bring wholeness to the psychological and emotional aspects of our person. Informed by a trinitarian understanding of creation, aspects of this wholeness can and do occur within the created realm. Because God created a world that is knowable to those who inquire, Christian psychologists can see part of their work as helping others to understand their own relational patterns and develop these to bring people into reconciliation with themselves and others.

Concluding Remarks

In this chapter we have argued that, from a Christian perspective, clinical psychology can be seen as a way to participate in God's project of bringing wholeness and healing to the human creatures whom God loves. This vision of clinical psychology turns on the theological claim that God's Spirit brings forth good things through psychology, whether a particular psychologist acknowledges this or not. As mentioned earlier, truth about the world is accessible through a practice like psychotherapy not because it proves the existence of God or explicitly discusses spiritual matters, but because God has ordered

33. Stolorow, Brandchaft, and Atwood, *Psychoanalytic Treatment*, 185.

a world that is knowable to the one who investigates and explores. This knowability includes behavioral patterns that can be discovered through psychotherapy. While psychology is the study of human thought and behavior, it can also be understood theologically as one way humans explore and shape creation. God has created humans with the unique ability to wonder, dream, and develop the created realm, and clinical psychology is one form that this kind of exploration and development takes. With this in mind, we offer a few points concerning how we might move the conversation forward regarding mental health and the church.

First, mental health diagnoses, while useful for mental health care professionals, should not be the only labels that define persons—whether in psychotherapy or in the church. Often, mental health diagnoses have been wrongly used to name persons rather than their behavior, and as John Swinton rightly notes, diagnostic categories do not tell us who a person is or help us understand the broader narrative that is the fabric of their life.[34] Complicating matters further, the inappropriate usage of diagnostic categories by nonprofessionals within the church often contributes to stigmatization and social suffering. When a mental health diagnosis becomes the only lens through which people are seen, these diagnostic labels contribute to a narrative about persons that perpetuates ostracization and enhances pessimism about recovery.[35]

In contradistinction to the diagnostic categories given by the fifth edition of the *Diagnostic and Statistical Manual of Mental Disorders*, Swinton suggests that the church should understand mental health issues as distinctive experiences that disrupt people's personal narratives and require care and respect, alongside rehabilitation and treatment.[36] According to Swinton, because there is a tendency for

34. We are indebted to Swinton and his article "Time, Hospitality, and Belonging" for this point and general direction for this section.

35. Language and the naming of creation matter. The Genesis text speaks to humanity's ability to name things, and this naming involves relationship. The naming of the plants and animals can be seen as a relational task as humanity enters into a certain kind of relationship with creation. For more on this, see Walter Brueggemann, *Genesis*, Interpretation: A Bible Commentary for Preaching and Teaching (Atlanta: John Knox, 1982).

36. Swinton, "Time, Hospitality, and Belonging," 171–81.

people not only to "have a diagnosis but to become a diagnosis," pastors and lay leaders should call for a moratorium on diagnostic mental health labels being used in the church community.[37] In regard to psychotherapists using diagnostic criteria, this of course is part of their job. But early career psychologists in particular must take care not to let diagnostic labels define persons in their entirety, and the Christian values of love, grace, and mercy must always guide our treatment protocols and relational dynamics no matter who a client might be or how they might be diagnosed.

Second, building on a point made earlier, it is the work of the Spirit to bring diverse realities and individuals together. This means that differences among members are not unbridgeable gaps that ultimately keep members of the body of Christ from entering into meaningful relationships with one another. Dignity and respect must be afforded to all people (both inside and outside the church), whether one has a mental health diagnosis or not. In fact, it is the Spirit who works to help others come into relationship with those perceived to be different—the misunderstood or marginalized—and this includes those struggling with mental illness. This movement of the Spirit to create a hospitable space for others is also a spiritual practice. As such, it must be embodied by Christians in order for it to become a felt reality. Embodying this kind of hospitality begins by confronting the ways in which we stigmatize others (consciously or not) whom we perceive as different. The spiritual practice of self-examination is valuable here. Who do we perceive as being of lesser value and why? And how might we work to extend honor specifically to those whom we perceive as different? Here, we must keep in mind that it is the work of the Spirit that enables us to create spaces of hospitality within ourselves, confronting our own shadows of discrimination and disbelief.

Third, while the Spirit helps us stay in contact with or move toward those whom we perceive as different, the Spirit also helps us recognize that we have something to learn from people with a mental health diagnosis. To use Gunton's terms, this is to recognize our dynamic interrelatedness. Think back to the story of schizophrenia described

37. Swinton, "Time, Hospitality, and Belonging," 174.

by anthropologist Juli McGruder. It was the community within which this person was embedded that either heightened or lessened the stigmatization of such a diagnosis. It's a profound example concerning the ways in which the views of a community can either bring acceptance or rejection to the people who make up that community—either aiding in their individual and corporate healing or facilitating further isolation.

This work of bringing together humans to be in relationship can be regarded as one way that the Spirit brings about unity and helps persons recognize the beauty of difference. While it can often be painful to embrace (or be embraced by) others who are perceived to be different, it is the necessary condition for those extending hospitality and for those receiving hospitality to experience transformation. Swinton notes that, within the church community, being hospitable to those with mental illness means that a space is created so that others in the church community may move toward understanding the deeper complexity of mental illness as a struggle that is both disruptive and yet holds potential for being meaningful.[38] If we take hospitality seriously, this means the church must take time to slow down and listen to these meaningful experiences of those with mental health issues. Our job is not to diagnose or reduce the person to some biological health issue that needs control or cure but to begin to listen and understand mental health problems "as important aspects of a person's life story."[39]

Embracing those with a mental health diagnosis means that we must be willing to practice spiritual disciplines like humility, empathy, and compassion in order to see the humanity of others and move toward them instead of consciously or unconsciously excluding them through stigmatizing behaviors. Creating spaces that might ease the social suffering of those with mental illness should not be thought of as an end in itself; rather, as Mary Oliver observes in a poem on prayer, we might think of it as a "doorway into thanks" and a quietness into which another voice may speak.[40]

---

38. Swinton, "Time, Hospitality, and Belonging," 181.
39. Swinton, "Time, Hospitality, and Belonging," 178.
40. See Mary Oliver's poem "Praying," in *Thirst* (Boston: Beacon, 2006), 37.

Questions for Reflection and Discussion

1. What has your experience with therapy been? If you have been shaped by a specific Christian tradition, how does that stream of Christianity approach mental health in general and psychotherapy in particular?

2. What do you think might happen if churches and religious leaders put a moratorium on using mental health diagnoses in the context of Christian community?

3. How does the psychological notion of inheriting destructive behavioral patterns that operate without our conscious awareness affect how you think about sin?

4. What have you learned about yourself by studying or working with persons who have mental health disorders? What else might they teach the community of faith about God, one another, or what it means to be human?

Resources for Reading and Exploration

McMinn, Mark R. *Sin and Grace in Christian Counseling: An Integrative Paradigm*. Downers Grove, IL: IVP Academic, 2008.

Swinton, John. *Becoming Friends of Time: Disability, Timefullness, and Gentle Discipleship*. Waco: Baylor University Press, 2016.

Watters, Ethan. *Crazy Like Us: The Globalization of the American Psyche*. New York: Free Press, 2011.

7

Psychology as Contextual Theology

Key takeaways from this chapter:

- As a person of Christian faith, to practice psychology is to engage in a form of contextual theology.
- God's future kingdom informs our present pursuit of justice and shalom in and through psychology.
- For people of Christian faith, hope is not optional.
- God's grace enables other virtues like justice and compassion to be fully realized.

Those of you who experienced the effects the economic downturn after the housing market crash in 2008 and the COVID-19 pandemic of 2020 know firsthand what it is like to see people losing their jobs and struggling to pay their rent. It may be that some of you couldn't find work or knew a friend or family member who lost their job and had to go on unemployment. If you were watching the news during 2020, most economic experts compared the decline of the economy in 2020 to the Great Depression in the late 1920s. However, most experts agree that while the initial decline of the economy in 2020 was sharper than the initial contraction of the economy during the Great Depression, the Great Depression lasted much longer and had much more devastating effects. To date, the Great Depression still stands as the most severe depression that has occurred in the industrialized Western world with crushing declines in employment that persisted over many years.[1]

The Great Depression started when the New York Stock Exchange crashed in 1929, sending Wall Street into a panic and wiping out billions in investments. Around the worst time of the Depression in New York, about a third of New York city workers were unemployed, and homeless encampments called Hoovervilles sprang up around the city for those who had lost their jobs and homes and were struggling just to stay alive.[2] Dorothy Day, a talented journalist who converted to Catholicism when she was about thirty, perceived that the church and government were doing an inadequate job of caring for the hungry and the homeless in the city. Drawing from the church's teaching that Jesus stood in solidarity with and cared for the poor, Day was committed to inspiring others to do the same. Using her journalistic skills, she began a newspaper, the *Catholic Worker*, with another social activist and Catholic theologian, Peter Maurin. Together they began to write about how we should all be committed to works of mercy and compassion for those who are immediately around us. This newspaper also highlighted systemic inequalities in the city and advocated for the poor, eventually inspiring a wide readership and what was to become known as the Catholic Worker Movement.

One of the chief outworkings of the movement were houses of hospitality, which involved people offering up their own houses to feed and serve the poor. Inspired by Day and Maurin's vision set forth in the *Catholic Worker* newspaper, these houses of hospitality were

1. David C. Wheelock, "Comparing the COVID-19 Recession with the Great Depression," *Economic Synopses* 29, 2020, https://doi.org/10.20955/es.2020.39.

2. Hoovervilles got their name from those who blamed President Herbert Hoover for the economic downturn that occurred during the Great Depression. See Pauline Toole, "Unemployment in the Great Depression," NYC Department of Records and Information Services, October 9, 2020, https://www.archives.nyc/blog/2020/10/9/9ovdpgn8lc5zxcild0ooltvzmfwx22.

started by ordinary women and men who put the teachings of Jesus into practical application through works of mercy such as feeding the hungry, giving drink to the thirsty, and sheltering the homeless.[3] The houses were supported through donations, and workers volunteered for short or long periods of time. For Day, everyone had a personal responsibility to help those in need, and knowing that workers could easily get discouraged by the amount of need around them, she would remind them that their primary concern was to be faithful in individual actions by focusing on one person at a time or one act of mercy at a time.[4] Just like the boy who offered up the loaves and fish in the Gospel narratives, Day told others that all they had to do was to be faithful and give what they had and that God would take it from there.[5] One day, after seeing the intolerable conditions of one of the makeshift homeless Hoovervilles and walking through the ankle-deep mud, Day reminded folks that "Christ is there . . . there in the mud, in the shacks with His poor."[6] Day's life and work embodied many of the key elements that are critical in helping professions like social work and psychology, but the primary animating principle for her vision was that human beings—no matter their race, background, or socioeconomic status—are created in the image of God and are thus worthy of dignity and respect. Day championed this cause and vision until her death in 1980.

Contextual Theology, Psychology, and a Vision for Human Flourishing

Dorothy Day is an inspiring and compelling example of someone practicing contextual theology. We noted earlier how we all practice theology from the context that we are embedded in, and we can never step outside this context, so all theology is, in fact, contextual. Whether it is our cultural and ethnic background or how we have

---

3. Coleman Fannin, "Dorothy Day's Radical Hospitality," in *Hospitality: Christian Reflection*, ed. Robert B. Kruschwitz (Waco: Baylor University Press, 2007), 37–45.

4. Fannin, "Dorothy Day's Radical Hospitality," in *Hospitality*, 42.

5. Dorothy Day, "Aims and Purposes," *Catholic Worker*, February 1940, 7.

6. Dorothy Day, "Hooverville," *Catholic Worker*, May 1940, 5.

been shaped by our studies in psychology, our sociohistorical location informs the way we see the world and how we live out our faith in that context. Day's life and work exemplify a woman who did just this. She took her skills, talents, and training in journalism and applied them to the context where she was embedded in New York. What started as a newspaper that sold for one cent grew into a movement that cast a vision for helping the poor. Day also embodied this vision by being with the poor and serving the poor in the hospitality houses.

However, it wasn't just Day's talents in journalism that started this movement; her faith provided the vision and the underlying motivation for what she should do. In other words, Day was a contextual theologian; that is, she practiced theology by letting her faith both inform and speak into her specific situation and context. With Day's example in mind, this chapter unfolds in light of four interrelated claims.

First, practicing theology is always an exercise of letting our faith inform what we are doing and why we are doing it. Theology isn't something that is reserved for those with PhDs in religion or something that only pastors, ministers, and priests do. Our theology and faith are motivated and informed by God's work in our world and the work of God in our lives. Being a theologian or practicing theology is simply the application of our own faith and God's love in a concrete situation. Theology is a lived practice; as a student of psychology who is also a person of faith, you will have the opportunity to let your faith inform the vision of what you do in your vocation within psychology.

Second, for the contextual theologian, the end informs the present. God's vision for humanity is one that has a certain telos—or end goal of restoration and healing (recall chap. 4). Letting our faith inform our work means that we are drawn in a certain direction. Knowing that Christ will draw all things to himself in the end and that God stands in solidarity with those who suffer gives us motivation, strength, and hope for the present. This was definitely true for Dorothy Day. Her vision of Christ's solidarity with the poor and the dignity of all humanity kept her grounded in the midst of enormous suffering. You can also think of this telos as the purpose or reason for doing what we are doing, which raises an interesting question, especially for people of Christian faith. What are the motivations or end goals that compel you to do what you are doing within your particular subdiscipline of psychology?

Third, just as Day upheld the dignity of human life and worked to cultivate shalom in the context she inhabited, you too will have an opportunity to allow the vision of God's love to bring wholeness and healing to the world in the context where you find yourself within the discipline of psychology. The underlying motivation and the end goal of the work we do should be centered around a desire to join the work of God to bring flourishing and shalom to our sphere of influence. Given the unique features of psychology, and that most social scientists are also on a quest for the improvement of human life, the theological notions of flourishing and shalom fit nicely within the psychological project, and in some cases provide it with a legitimacy it otherwise doesn't possess. The Christian confession of Christ as Lord moves us beyond the walls of the church to reflect and imagine how Christ's work would make a difference for the society, culture, and neighborhoods in which we live and move and have our being.

Fourth, Day's life and ministry highlight the importance of certain Christian virtues in the specific work she was doing. Day's vision was inspired by Christian compassion, hospitality, and mercy. There will, of course, be certain theological virtues that inform our action (i.e., ethics) regardless of the situation in which we find ourselves. However, within the realm of psychology, there are a few theological virtues that can and should inform our work in particular: justice, love, hope, grace, and hospitality. By reflecting on these virtues, we are able to see how they can inform and enhance our work in psychology and give shape to the various contexts in which we have been placed.

Much of this book has focused on clarifying and expounding the underlying theological motivations for operating within one or more of the various psychological subdisciplines. We have gone so far as to suggest that God's work in the world can be carried out through human involvement in clinical and research psychology, and that God's Spirit enables us to participate as co-laborers in God's creative work, thus allowing us to contribute to the wholeness and healing of individuals and communities through research or clinical work—or both. In the previous chapters we've demonstrated how, as

Christians, psychological scientific research is always interpreted from a larger theological framework that is informed by our faith, culture, experience, and background. For the remainder of this chapter, we demonstrate how justice, love, hope, grace, and hospitality have the potential to serve as an ethical framework that can guide the ways in which psychological practitioners who are also Christ-followers respond to the specific contexts in which they are embedded.

Justice

For Christians, the biblical idea of justice is rooted in a God who is just and a God who stands against human sin and human oppression. Just as the theme of God's love runs throughout Scripture (insofar as God remains faithfully committed to creation and to humanity), so does the theme of justice. Not only does God consistently stand against those things that destroy humanity, but God also desires the human community to be an example of God's mercy and love.

The two Hebrew words that biblical authors most commonly use to describe the idea of justice in the Hebrew Scriptures are *mispat* and *sedaqah*. These words often occur together as a pair in the Old Testament prophetic books and are commonly translated as "justice" and "righteousness."[7] According to Old Testament scholar and theologian Walter Brueggemann, when the prophets called for justice and righteousness they were referring to an order in human society that is viable and sustainable—one in which neighbors can dwell in solidarity with one another.[8] In the New Testament, God's justice is embodied in Jesus Christ, who expresses care for those who are marginalized and on the outskirts of society. Luke 4 (as we've already noted) is a proclamation of God's justice on earth. Jesus is the harbinger of justice through his provision of bodily restoration, proclaiming freedom for those imprisoned and offering freedom to those who are oppressed. Remember from chapter 4 that there are both proximate and ultimate areas of existence. God's justice addresses both areas. In the proximate areas, God stands with those who are marginalized

7. Walter Brueggemann, *God, Neighbor, Empire: The Excess of Divine Fidelity and the Command of Common Good* (Waco: Baylor University Press, 2016), 12.
    8. Brueggemann, *God, Neighbor, Empire*, 13, 40.

and calls us to dismantle unjust systems that cause oppression, and in the ultimate areas, God assures us that justice will be administered in the end when all humanity stands before God.

It is important to point out that each of these biblical concepts (whether it be the poor and oppressed, or righteousness and restoration) is describing a concrete reality, and justice is no exception. Notice that God's justice always moves toward action, whether it is through the prophets or Jesus. Just like love, there is an action-oriented element to justice. God's justice flows from God's love and desire for righteousness. And most importantly for our work here, there is always an element of human agency involved, as God desires humans to live out and practice justice in their lives at both the individual and communal levels. Ultimately, we cannot just talk about justice but must act in ways that promote and uphold justice in the areas where we have influence.

Consequently, as Christians working in the field of psychology, our work should be informed by the Christian faith's understanding of justice as an act of loving solidarity that addresses the material concerns of those who have been marginalized or oppressed. In order to be truly loving, we not only have to call evil what it is but we must also use our position to help elevate the dignity of those who suffer. This kind of justice can take many forms in research and psychotherapy, but at the very least it involves acting in ways that are within the bounds of ethical and legal guidelines. It's hard to imagine us advocating for justice without at least starting from an ethical place that licensing boards and standards of practice require. But, of course, the hope is that we will move well beyond the bare minimum. From our perspective, ethical practices within psychology that are informed by a Christian understanding of justice can take three forms: (1) advocating for justice, (2) understanding the injustices experienced by marginalized groups or individuals in research or clinical work, and (3) working to eradicate injustices in organizations and in the lives of individuals.

As indicated in the previous chapter, we must also understand that certain groups have experienced the trauma of injustice more than other groups, which means that justice-oriented work is often corrective. Black, Brown, Indigenous groups, and other persons of color have experienced both systemic oppression and intergenerational trauma from injustices. Women and LGBTQ individuals are also not strangers to injustices, discrimination, and trauma. As Christians, we cannot be naive about these dynamics, especially as it concerns the extreme vulnerability of those who embody the intersection of multiple marginalized identities. White researchers and psychotherapists in particular must do their own work to understand these dynamics in order to advocate for and work toward eradicating injustices for marginalized groups. We also must do our due diligence practicing incarnational psychology by being with others—not in the form of solving or advice-giving but by listening, being humble, and sitting with others in pain. For those who identify as White, the work of justice also means that we examine and become familiar with our privileges and how we live in a system that has granted an easier time for those who are White than for persons of color (and the same can also be said for those who identify as heterosexual, cisgendered men in comparison to others).

Injustices can occur on a systemic level (among groups), relational level (between persons), intrapsychic level (within individuals), or incorporate elements from all three of these levels simultaneously. Disparity in the allocation of resources is a frequent injustice that occurs with respect to marginalized groups and would be an example of systemic injustice. Advocating for justice in this realm might mean dedicating a portion of your therapy practice, time, or research to eradicating this form of injustice. It could be as simple as allocating some of your time in clinical practice to seeing clients at a low fee or no fee. Or, within research, it could mean dedicating a portion of your research to understanding more about and working to correct some of these health disparities.

On an individual and intrapsychic level, psychotherapists frequently encounter injustices in how people view themselves, or hear about injustices that have occurred between persons. Psychotherapy is a unique place where we can point out these injustices and can also work to equip people to address injustices within their own lives. For example, some people might be unaware of the violence they express to themselves in their own self-talk, and eradicating injustice on this personal level might look something like providing alternative ways of thinking about themselves and offering a different narrative stressing self-worth instead of dismissiveness or shame. At the end of the day, the specific ways in which each of us responds to these injustices will depend on the unique demands of our individual contexts, but the common thread that unites all our efforts is a shared commitment to God's compassionate care for the marginalized and oppressed.

Love

The English word for "love" has a broad range of meanings. We use the same word ("love") to describe all manner of relationships, from things that we really like, to causes or people that we would dedicate ourselves to or even die for. We say we love a new Netflix show, or love our lover, or love our dog, or love our mother. In reality, each of these uses of the word "love" actually means something slightly different, depending on what or whom our love is directed toward. If I (William) told you "I absolutely *love* Ben and Jerry's half-baked cookie dough ice cream," you know I just mean that I really, really like it. You probably know that I wouldn't sacrifice my life for a pint of Ben and Jerry's or put my son's life on the line for some Ben and Jerry's. (Though I do think my wife might put *my* life on the line for some Ben and Jerry's—we're still working through that in therapy.) Even though we use the word "love" to describe our enjoyment of inanimate objects, we also use the same English word to describe the relational love that connects us to other people and to God. Thus, when we use the word "love" in this relational sense, we are often using it to describe a deep commitment, care, and respect for our family, a spouse, or a romantic partner.

In contrast, the Hebrew word for love carries a rich meaning. *Hesed* describes a deep steadfast love that remains committed no matter what. It's a love that is self-sacrificing and oriented toward others. For instance, as expressed in Jeremiah 31:3, God's love is steadfast, long-lasting, and committed to seeing Israel flourish and thrive: "I have loved you with an everlasting love; I have drawn you with unfailing kindness" (NIV). From a theological perspective, justice and love go hand in hand. God is against those things that destroy humanity and human dignity (the theological foundations for justice) because of God's deep and steadfast love for the world God created. In the

New Testament, we are reminded that, first and foremost, God is love (1 John 4:8) and that love is the "greatest" of Christian virtues, rising above both faith and hope (1 Cor. 13:13). *Agape* is the Greek work that best captures this form of self-sacrificing and unconditional love. In 1 Corinthians 13, Paul reminds us that love never fails. Moreover, the first and greatest commandment as paraphrased by Jesus is to love God, and the second greatest commandment is to love our neighbor as ourselves (Matt. 22:36–40). The commandment to love our neighbor as ourself brings us back to our discussion in chapter 4, where we suggested that self-love is intimately bound up with our ability to love others.

If you've had some exposure to Christianity, then the notion that "God is love" is an idea with which you are likely already familiar. Although the theological basis for love is found in God's own self, love is action oriented. God moved to create the world out of love and remains committed to humanity and that world. Moreover, the movement of God's love extends to human love so that we are called to act in a loving way toward our neighbor. We know from attachment theory in psychology that lives devoid of a solid, loving attachment figure early in life may struggle later to form deep and lasting relationships. Love remains the bond that binds us to God and binds us to one another as a human community. And, as difficult as it may seem, the radical claim of Jesus is that love is to be extended not only toward those whom we know and like but also toward our enemies (Matt. 5:42–43).

When viewed from this perspective, it may very well be that our work in psychotherapy and psychological research is best understood as an act of love. Operating with an ethic of love shapes our purposes and motivations as practitioners of psychology. In addition, it directs and guides the way we relate to others. Being motivated by God's love helps ground us when we work with clients who have difficult presenting issues or when we encounter challenges in our own families. Love helps us remember that when people express anger, fear, or frustration, our primary task is to empathize with them and extend grace to them.

Psychotherapists often act as an embodied (and incarnated) form of love for clients or patients, and through their creation of hospitable spaces healing can and does occur. When we consider that we have the ability to shape and tend to the created realm, we also see that our work within psychology is a way to nurture other people. Relationships that have been neglected or shaped by hatred, violence, and greed lead to the diminishment rather than the enhancement of human personhood. Conversely, relationships that are carefully nurtured through love over time have the potential to thrive. Indeed, the sheer resilience of the human person is a testament to the restorative effects of this kind of relational love.

Hope

Hope is a robust concept within the Christian tradition, one that carries with it numerous ramifications for anyone working in psychology from the perspective of faith. Echoing Paul's discussion of the Christian virtues of "faith, hope, and love" in 1 Corinthians 13, Thomas Aquinas, the premier theologian of the Roman Catholic Church, regarded hope as a theological virtue (along with faith and love). Aquinas noted that hope is different from human optimism since it relies on a future that is established by God.[9] Christian hope pursues good even though it might be hard to find, in large part because it is activated and animated by the self-giving love of God and the grace of Christ.[10] Following this line of thought, Jürgen Moltmann's landmark work, *Theology of Hope*, moved eschatology (the study of the last things and the future life with God) and hope to the center of twentieth-century theological discourse. For Moltmann, hope is the power of the future reality of God's new kingdom: a future life with God that bears upon our present reality.[11] Though we might not always see it, the world is being drawn toward this new reality, which was established through the death and resurrection of Christ. For Moltmann, knowing that our future reality is established

9. Thomas Aquinas, *Summa Theologica*, II-II.17–22.

10. Douglas Meeks, "Hope," in *The Cambridge Dictionary of Christian Theology*, ed. Ian A. McFarland, David A. S. Fergusson, Karen Kilby, and Iain R. Torrance (New York: Cambridge University Press, 2011), 225–26.

11. Jürgen Moltmann, *Theology of Hope: On the Ground and the Implications of a Christian Eschatology* (Minneapolis: Fortress, 1993), 91.

by God is the foundational element of hope, and it is on the basis of this eschatological hope that we pursue justice and righteousness in the here and now.[12]

With theologians like Aquinas, and even Moltmann, hope is conceptualized differently than it is in positive psychology. Although positive psychology's theoretical and empirical explorations provide us with helpful insights regarding the underlying psychological processes of hope, in the psychology literature hope is grounded in human action, not God's action. Moreover, research on hope in positive psychology is goal-oriented, but it posits human volition alone as the ultimate motivation for moving the self toward a desired goal. This operative assumption leads psychologists Kevin Rand and Kaitlin Touza to define hope as the ability to produce "pathways to achieve desired goals and to motivate oneself to use those pathways."[13] Again, there is much to learn from these psychological and anthropocentric descriptions of hope, but both Aquinas and Moltmann underscore the transcendent character of hope as being grounded in God's action to save, redeem, and restore. God is ultimately the one who assures the future kingdom of peace will come about. Or, as Mark McMinn puts it, hope connects persons with the purposes of God that extend beyond the self.[14]

The Christian virtue of hope pursues the good because we trust and know that, ultimately, God leads and guides us in the present and assures a future reality of restoration established through the death and resurrection of Christ. God not only loves both human and nonhuman creation in an ultimate sense but also desires for restoration and wholeness to come about in part in this present life. Christian hope is therefore not a futile or empty optimism, nor is it a naive refusal to acknowledge the suffering and pain that is present in the world. This kind of hard-won hope matters a great deal for the work we do in psychology because it enables us to stay grounded

12. Richard Bauckham, *The Theology of Jürgen Moltmann* (New York: T&T Clark, 1995), 39.

13. Kevin L. Rand and Kaitlin K. Touza, "Hope Theory," in *The Oxford Handbook of Positive Psychology*, ed. C. R. Snyder, S. J. Lopez, L. M. Edwards, and S. C. Marques, 3rd ed. (New York: Oxford University Press, 2009), 425.

14. Mark R. McMinn, *The Science of Virtue: Why Positive Psychology Matters to the Church* (Grand Rapids: Brazos, 2017), 5–6.

when we encounter human suffering rather than retreating from it or spiritualizing it away. It is for this very reason that Lisa Cahill proposes in *Global Justice, Christology and Christian Ethics* that hope cannot exist without justice. Hope is nurtured when justice is done, and our active work to bring about justice draws us closer to God and, in turn, nurtures hope.[15]

Consequently, Christian hope helps psychological practitioners encounter suffering and pursue justice without being completely consumed by it. There will be times in your work in psychology when you encounter human suffering. As psychotherapists, researchers, and professors, we encounter some degree of human suffering on almost a daily basis, and sometimes we must hold on to hope for clients or colleagues or students who haven't the capacity to hope, just as we need people to hold on to hope for us when we're in moments of despair or sadness. It is in those moments when we encounter human suffering that a fully orbed Christian hope allows us (as either a psychotherapist or researcher) to sit in the midst of suffering and to stay present with someone else. Hope allows us to seek the good and act justly. And for the person of Christian faith, this is not optional. Indeed, as Zechariah 9:12 reminds us, we are "prisoners of hope" (NIV).

Grace

While the word "grace" is used in everyday conversation to denote an extension of goodwill between persons (e.g., a grace period, or extending grace to someone), the Christian concept of grace has broad and rich contours that are rooted in the triune God's relationship with creation and the human creature. Within Scripture, grace can be understood as unmerited divine favor—the gift of a benevolent and loving God. Jesus is the one on whom God's grace resides (Luke 2:40), and Jesus is also the one who gives grace to others through his life, death, and resurrection (John 1:16).

We have addressed some of the types and qualities of grace in previous chapters. There is a common grace that God bestows on all of creation, indicating that God gives good things to all people even

---

15. Lisa Sowle Cahill, *Global Justice, Christology and Christian Ethics*, New Studies in Christian Ethics (Cambridge: Cambridge University Press, 2013), 6.

though they might not acknowledge God. Grace is also at the heart of salvation and restoration, the only means by which humans can be rescued from their sinful condition and brought into communion with God. It is also important to remember that if God was acting completely justly, no human would be able to be in communion with God. So it is God's grace that makes it possible for a relationship with the Creator to exist in the first place, and it is in and through Jesus Christ that God's grace and love have been freely given to us (Rom. 3:24; 5:8).

Theologians have hotly debated the mechanics by which grace is bestowed on the human person (is it imputed or infused?) and have also arrived at different conclusions regarding how grace works in a person's life before someone comes to acknowledge Christ (see chap. 2 on prevenient grace). Entering into these centuries-long conversations is part of doing theology, but we haven't the space to fully unpack them here. In our estimation, the most important point to remember is that we are undeserving of God's grace, and yet it is freely given to us by God. Every breath of air that we take, every moment of goodness that we encounter in our day, our week, our life, indeed, our very existence, are possible only because we live in a state of being changed and transformed in light of the reality of God's grace.

As constructive theologians, we have both inherited our theological sensibilities from the Protestant tradition of Christianity. In addition to this, I (William) find Eastern Orthodox notions of grace quite compelling. The Eastern Orthodox Church has historically understood grace as the energy that flows forth from the persons of the Trinity, which has a transformative effect on everything that it encounters.[16] Grace is the energy of God that draws us into God's life, enables us to participate in the life of God, and brings about life.[17] Some Orthodox theologians compare grace to the rays of the sun that both warm and change anything they encounter.

The recognition that we have received these transformative rays of life-giving energy from God leaves us with little other choice than

16. Vladimir Lossky, *The Mystical Theology of the Eastern Church* (Cambridge: Lutterworth Press, 1957), 75–86.

17. Wolfhart Pannenberg, *Systematic Theology*, trans. G. W. Bromiley (Grand Rapids: Eerdmans, 1997), 3:197–98.

to respond with gratitude for what has been received.[18] And it is this seemingly inexorable move toward thanksgiving that has immediate implications for our work and actions within psychology. Just as the light of the sun shining on a garden enables all kinds of plants and other things to grow, the energy of God's grace helps cultivate or "grow" other virtues or strengths. As McMinn rightly notes, when we extend kindness to others, some might call this grace, but this kindness or goodness is still qualitatively different from God's grace as it is given to us.[19] Even though, as humans, we do not dole out God's grace, we can understand grace as being the energy that enables other strengths like kindness, goodness, mercy, and compassion to be cultivated in our own life. God's grace helps us make space for others and enables us to cultivate other virtues like empathy, compassion, and gratitude as we work with clients in psychotherapy.

We can also understand God's grace as being present in how we go about study and research, creating an environment that allows us to foster self-acceptance and self-compassion.[20] By allowing ourselves to be mindfully aware of the divine grace that is freely given to us, we are able to create transformative spaces that provide opportunities for us to understand and accept the strengths and shortcomings of ourselves and others.[21] As we become more aware of God's grace, we are able to practice compassion for others and for ourselves. Again, God's grace is the energy or life force that enables other virtues like compassion (for self and others) to grow. And as Kristen Neff notes, self-compassion involves a kindness toward ourselves, a remembrance of being part of a common or shared humanity where we all have imperfections, and being mindful of painful thoughts and feelings without overidentifying with them.[22] Grace is a vital ingredient not only for the work we do with others but also for the work we do with ourselves.

18. Robert A. Emmons, Peter C. Hill, Justin L. Barrett, and Kelly M. Kapic, "Psychological and Theological Reflections on Grace and Its Relevance for Science and Practice," *Psychology of Religion and Spirituality* 9, no. 3 (2017): 276–84.

19. McMinn, *The Science of Virtue*, 147–48.

20. Emmons et al., "Psychological and Theological Reflections," 280.

21. Emmons et al., "Psychological and Theological Reflections," 280.

22. Kristen Neff, "Self-Compassion: An Alternative Conceptualization of a Healthy Attitude Toward Oneself," *Self and Identity* 2, no. 2 (2003): 85–101.

Hospitality

Throughout the history of the Christian church, the practice of hospitality, or welcoming the stranger, has been regarded as an extension of God's grace to others.[23] In this way, it is appropriate to talk about hospitality after we have discussed grace. For instance, in *Untamed Hospitality: Welcoming God and Other Strangers*, theologian Elizabeth Newman writes about the connection between grace and hospitality: "Our lives are always gifts of God; the divine spring continually supplies what we need. There is never a time when we can sit back and say, 'Ahh, now my life is mine.' Such a way of thinking distorts not only our lives but more fundamentally the nature of God, whose superabundant giving never ceases because it lies at the heart of God's triune identity."[24] Here, Newman helpfully points out that the ability for us to give to others and to strangers is because God's grace never stops being given to us.

The roots of the Christian practice of hospitality come from the Hebrew Scriptures and draw from Israel's experience of being enslaved by the Egyptians. Exodus 23:9 states that the stranger should not be oppressed because "you [Israel] know the heart of a stranger, for you were strangers in the land of Egypt" (RSV). A similar command is repeated in Deuteronomy 10:19: "Love the sojourner therefore; for you were sojourners in the land of Egypt" (RSV). These commandments inspire the teachings found in Matthew 25:35 where Jesus reminds us that welcoming the stranger by providing food, drink, or clothes is the same as welcoming him. What is often missed in this text is how Jesus elevates the worth and dignity of those who are on the margins. Jesus specifically mentions those who are in prison, those who are sick, those who do not have food, drink, or clothes, and those who are otherwise outsiders (strangers). These people too, says Jesus, are sacred in the eyes of God, and are worthy of being welcomed and provided for. Paul continues a similar line of reasoning in Romans 12 by encouraging the Christians in the Roman church to "practice hospitality" (Rom. 12:13 RSV), indicating that even our

---

23. Donald K. McKim, "Hospitality," in *The Westminster Dictionary of Theological Terms*, 2nd ed. (Louisville: Westminster John Knox, 2014).

24. Elizabeth Newman, *Untamed Hospitality: Welcoming God and Other Strangers*, The Christian Practice of Everyday Life (Grand Rapids: Brazos, 2007), 170.

enemies should be given food and drink in this radical practice of overcoming evil with good (Rom. 12:20).

Darrell Guder, in his book *Missional Church*, describes the Christian practice of hospitality as the way we as humans participate in God's "peaceable kingdom." Guder notes, "Such hospitality indicates the crossing of boundaries (ethnic origin, economic condition, political orientation, gender status, social experience, educational background) by being open and welcoming of the other. Without such communities of hospitality, the world will have no way of knowing that all God's creation is meant to live in peace."[25]

Hospitality comes to bear on our actions as Christians and psychologists when we consider the act of welcoming those on the margins as a means for pursuing justice. Hospitality is a way to peaceably "host" those who feel like outsiders because of their race, mental status, sexual orientation, or economic status. In my work as a therapist, I (William) see time and time again how clients bring parts of themselves out into the open, hoping that these parts will be welcomed and seen, that is, granted hospitality. When we have experiences in life in which we are clearly not welcome and are instead shamed because of who we are, the result is that we begin to hide these parts of ourselves. However, hiding merely prevents us from bringing these aspects of ourselves out into the open so that we might understand them. We need to be around others who are able to graciously and hospitably hold these parts of ourselves because we cannot begin to change what we cannot see or understand. Psychotherapy offers such a hospitable space for exactly this kind of change to begin: a space where we might take those first steps toward being and becoming whole.

From Hospitality to Wholeness

In the contemporary, largely capitalist context, hospitality is often seen in purely transactional terms. It's either a "service" that comes with the purchase of some other commodity (like a hotel's concierge service), or the name for an entire industry of for-profit businesses

25. Darrell L. Guder, ed., *Missional Church: A Vision for the Sending of the Church in North America*, The Gospel and Our Culture (Grand Rapids: Eerdmans, 1998), 5–6.

ranging anywhere from restaurants and hotels to amusement parks and casinos. This service-oriented notion does make some sense given that the English word "hospitality" is drawn from the Latin adjective *hospitalis*, meaning "of a guest." Interestingly, the Latin root for this word (*hospes*) is also where we get the English words "hospital," "hostel," "hotel," and "host." All these words indicate a sense of being open to those who are in need of a place to stay or looking for help. But it is also the case that *hospes* is formed from the word *hostis*, which means "stranger" or "enemy." It's where we derive English words like "hostile" and "hostage." So hospitality cannot be simply about opening up a space where friends and other like-minded folks gather—people who we know will reciprocate either in the form of some kind of currency or by returning the favor at a later time. Rather, hospitality in the thick sense—the Christian sense—is about opening up our most intimate of spaces to those we know full well might never repay us or, worse yet, might seek to do us harm.

Jesus continually reminded his listeners that anyone can extend love and compassion to those who already love us (Matt. 5:43–48). But the kingdom that Jesus was sent to proclaim demands something of us that is far more radical: loving our enemies. It's one thing to demonstrate grace and hospitality to those we expect will treat us with an equal measure of kindness and respect. It's something else altogether to take that same risk of hospitality without any such assurances. This is not to say that clinical psychologists who are people of Christian faith should be reckless with respect to the clients they serve or take unnecessary risks that might put themselves or others in harm's way. Some level of risk is, of course, always involved when working with human beings, but Jesus isn't implying that we should entirely abandon wisdom and discernment. Rather, Jesus is suggesting that hospitality necessarily involves some level of disruption and discomfort on the part of the host.

Hospitality is not about making ourselves and others comfortable; it's about allowing others to change us. It's about moving toward a form of wholeness that is deeply relational, which means that it is nothing if not a messy and risk-filled endeavor. It isn't simply about the restoration and well-being of others (although that's a big part of it); it's about the transformation of our own selves and the broader niche we inhabit along with a diverse community of others who are both like and unlike us. Indeed, there is a real risk in showing genuine hospitality. The host might encounter another human being in all their brokenness and all their difference and, as a result, be forever changed. Quite understandably, it's a risk not everyone is willing to take. But for those who are willing, of one thing we are certain: they will never be the same, and neither will the people whom they serve.

Questions for Reflection and Discussion

1. How might the concept of grace inform the work you envision doing in psychology?

2. Are there any limits to the hospitality that therapists should demonstrate toward their clients? If so, what might those limits be?

3. How would you describe the specific context in which you are called to provide mental health services? What are some of the challenges this context presents?

4. In practical terms, what does it mean for a clinical psychologist to hope on behalf of those who have lost the ability to do so?

Resources for Reading and Exploration

Cahill, Lisa Sowle. *Global Justice, Christology and Christian Ethics.* New Studies in Christian Ethics. Cambridge: Cambridge University Press, 2013.

McMinn, Mark R. *The Science of Virtue: Why Positive Psychology Matters to the Church.* Grand Rapids: Brazos, 2017.

Newman, Elizabeth. *Untamed Hospitality: Welcoming God and Other Strangers.* The Christian Practice of Everyday Life. Grand Rapids: Brazos, 2007.

Conclusion

What is the kingdom of God like? To what should I compare it? It is like a mustard seed that a man took and sowed in his garden. It grew and became a tree, and the wild birds nested in its branches.

—Luke 13:18–19

Not too long ago, I (Kutter) visited Apricot Lane, a farm just outside of Los Angeles County started in 2011 by Molly and John Chester. At the end of the guided tour, which featured a farm-to-table lunch, I realized that I had just experienced something wildly subversive. It wasn't simply that John and Molly's approach to regenerative farming embodied a critique of the large-scale monoculture that characterizes modern industrial agriculture. Rather, like an unassuming little seed lying dormant under an otherwise lifeless landscape, the subversion was planted much deeper, hidden beneath the soil.

Of course, at first blush, you wouldn't know it. Apricot Lane is nothing short of an endearing homage to all that's right with rural life. What's more, it's super cute. From the meticulously manicured

Portions of this conclusion were adapted from Kutter Callaway, "The Biggest Little Farm: A Parable of the Kingdom," Fuller Studio, https://fullerstudio.fuller.edu/the-biggest-little-farm-a-parable-of-the-kingdom. Used with permission.

garden to the expertly designed orchards and newborn lambs tram-
pling the ground beneath the lemon trees, it's something straight
out of a *Chic & Country* magazine spread. But follow Molly and
John behind the doors of the farm's fertility center and a whole new
world of soil and worms and micro-organisms unfolds. Suddenly,
the former private chef (Molly) and documentary filmmaker (John)
are no longer a couple who simply chose to leave the city behind for
a more whimsical and less hurried life in the country. Rather, they
are evangelists preaching the gospel of regenerative soil, biomimicry,
nutrient-dense foods, and, above all else, ecological interconnected-
ness. Oh, and as they hold aloft handfuls of microbe-rich soil from
their vermicomposting bins, it becomes clear that they also have a
deep and abiding passion for worm poop.

Every nook and cranny of Apricot Lane embodies John and Molly's undying commitment to the health of the soil and, by extension,
the vitality of the earth as a whole. But something else is going on just
beneath the surface. If you stop, look, and listen long enough, you
just might catch a glimpse of it. For instance, when my nine-year-old
daughter asked John how to tell the difference between a plant and
a weed, he offered up a piece of wisdom borne from the intimate
relationship he had cultivated with the land over the preceding eight
years of trial and travail: "There really is no such thing as a 'weed.'
That's just a name some people give to plants that are growing where
they don't want them to grow. But whatever you call them, they're a
sign of an imbalance in the land, and they invite us to a deeper form
of collaboration with the land."

It's a piece of wisdom that is profoundly simple but, at the very
same time, world-shattering. Indeed, although John and Molly don't
profess any kind of Christian faith, the lived wisdom they have stum-
bled on by simply observing the structure and workings of the created
order is strikingly similar to the sage advice that was spoken long ago
by a teacher who was also quite fond of pastoral metaphors: Jesus.

The suggestion that two people who do not profess to be followers
of Jesus could tap into the same stream of wisdom as Jesus might
come as a bit of a surprise for some, but not for readers of this book.
After all, Jesus himself rooted his life and teachings in the Hebrew
wisdom tradition—a way of life grounded in careful observation of

the created order. From Jesus's perspective, to pursue wisdom was to pursue that which had been present since the dawn of creation (Prov. 8:22) and was woven into the fabric of the natural order (Prov. 3:19). It was readily available to anyone who had the eyes to see it. Like farmers (both ancient and modern), artists, philosophers, and psychological scientists, Jesus was able to come to a deeper and more abiding understanding of God by examining the created order.

But Jesus didn't simply regurgitate the wisdom he inherited; he got creative with it. He told parables—world-changing, paradigm-shattering, topsy-turvy stories about the kingdom of God. Imagine that. Jesus was the fullest manifestation of God's revelatory presence in human history, and of all the ways he could have communicated with us about the coming kingdom, he chose to tell stories—stories about seeds, and birds, and trees, and unplowed fields, and baking bread. In other words, Jesus told stories about the everyday, mundane elements of pastoral life. His parables focused on farming and cooking and dealing with livestock, but they always had a twist that reoriented (or perhaps disoriented) his listeners. In these stories, extravagant parties are thrown for foolish and ungrateful sons. Entire flocks are abandoned to find a single wayward sheep. Wedding guests who fail to RSVP are uninvited to make room for the outcasts living on the margins of society. And mustard seeds are planted, growing into trees in which birds are able to nest.

When it comes to how the hard-won wisdom of a regenerative farmer relates to clinical and research psychology, the mustard seed parable is particularly illuminating, but not for the reasons one might imagine. Jesus's listeners, connected as they were to the land, would have immediately caught the scandalous nature of his parable. In the first place, they would have known that mustard plants don't grow large enough to support birds, so at the very least, Jesus's parable would have been understood as a rhetorical exaggeration, a way of highlighting the extravagant nature of the kingdom.

Perhaps even more important, though, mustard plants were also incredibly fast-growing and could take over a field in a brief period of time. In other words, they were weeds. Or at least that's the name they were given by those who sought to control the land and dominate it by forcing it to produce only one kind of crop. The consequences of such a label are far reaching and dire, fundamentally shifting the relationships between the land, the plant, and the farmer. Indeed, by diagnosing a broader ecological problem as entirely the fault of an individual plant, and then giving that diagnosis a name (i.e., a "weed"), the farmer is left with almost no other choice but to rip it out and kill it.

But as I learned from Molly and John while traveling with them through the biodynamic orchards of Apricot Lane Farms, there really is no such thing as a weed—at least not when the farmer's aim is to collaborate with the land so that it yields life rather than coerce the land into the production of goods. There are, of course, certain plants that run the risk of choking out others in the garden, but that's not because they are "weeds." That's because the land itself is crying out. When a particular plant has run amok, it is both a sign and symptom of a deeper and more pervasive imbalance in the ecosystem.

Odds are at least part of the reason you decided to study psychology and consider a career as a clinical psychologist or psychological scientist is because you recognized at some point in your life that things are not the way they should be and that it doesn't have to be this way (because it hasn't always been this way). It's also likely that, whether you were originally prompted by a sense of disjointedness in your own lived experience or by the voice of the land and its inhabitants crying out, you are now at a place where you desire to help address the mental, emotional, and behavioral imbalances that seem to plague so much of contemporary life. Given the pervasiveness of these psychological imbalances, we have talked at great length about the ways in which a constructive theology might aid students of psychology in their efforts to cultivate for themselves and others a space in which they might flourish. Indeed, because theology and psychology have so much to say about what is broken, pathological, and in need of healing, we intentionally focused much of our discussion on the ultimate ends to which both aim, a telos marked by God's life-giving presence.

It does no one any good to pretend the vision of wholeness and shalom that the Christian theological tradition articulates has been fully realized in the here and now, especially given the level, depth, and expanse of human suffering that has come to define reality for many people who are forced to navigate the various economic uncertainties, personal catastrophes, and global crises of the contemporary social order. God's redemptive project in the world is "already but not yet," and it is in the "not yet" that we most assuredly live. Creation groans as if in childbirth (Rom. 8:22) because it is not yet free of its bondage to decay and death, the defeat of which Christ began when God raised him from the dead but which will not be brought to completion until the day when God is all in all (1 Cor. 15:24–28).

Put a bit differently, theology and psychology share a common starting point: the catastrophic. We always begin in the chaos and crises and traumas of the world as it has been handed to us. Neither psychology nor theology can explain human suffering any more than they can explain it away. But it is always there, constituting the conditions of our existence, even when we are not consciously aware of its presence. We cannot ignore it or sublimate it or spiritualize it; we have no other choice but to reckon with it. Case in point: we have written almost the entirety of this book in the midst of a fourteen-month-long lockdown in Southern California due to a global pandemic that, at the time of this writing, has killed over half a million American citizens. During this same period of time, our region of the world also suffered historic wildfires that destroyed countless homes and displaced numerous families, including my (Kutter's) own. What is more, nationwide demonstrations protesting police brutality toward Black and Brown persons sparked a global reckoning about racial injustices that has been centuries in the making. The result of these overlapping catastrophes is a frayed and fraying national psyche, the full implications of which will not soon be known, much less understood. The only thing that we do know with crystal clarity is that the suffering and loss are not evenly distributed. Whether the active agent is a virus, an increase in global temperatures, or the systemic and structural racism of Western societies, the victims of all this trauma are overwhelmingly and disproportionately members of marginalized groups.

As it concerns our work as psychologists, our response to the various mental, emotional, and behavioral imbalances triggered by these cascading crises could take a number of forms. One way to respond would be to name their underlying "pathologies" in such a way that we have no other choice but to pluck them out at their roots, removing them permanently from what we believe to be an otherwise life-giving environment. Another approach would be to get creative and respond humbly to that which we must acknowledge is always already out of our control, recognizing that the imbalances produced by contemporary life are invitations to form a deeper and more intimate relationship with the land and one another.

Drawing on the insights of biodynamic farming, we might even say that to participate as psychologists in the kingdom Jesus inaugurated is to altogether cease from naming perceived threats as "weeds" in need of uprooting and instead create spaces and cultivate soils that will allow all plants to flourish and grow. Indeed, it may very well be that, in the coming kingdom, there simply is no such thing as a weed, not because life is easy or without thorns, but because every living thing has a vital role to play. And if this is truly the case, then it requires us to adopt not only a new way of seeing the world, but a new set of eyes.

To see the world in this way—with kingdom-oriented eyes—is to look at the beautiful complexity of our life in the natural order, which can be harsh and unforgiving, and see that it is alive with infinite possibility. It is to envision both the world and the complicated human beings in it the same way John and Molly see the human and nonhuman life on their land. As farmers, they look at the coyote and see an ally against gophers instead of a killer of chickens; they look at maggot-filled cow dung and see an excellent source of chicken feed rather than a fly infestation; they look at a plot of land an hour outside of LA and see the site of a regenerative farm instead of a dry and barren wasteland. And as John says, "When I look at it like that, it's perfect." What if we did the same? What if we saw those who struggle with depression or schizophrenia or eating disorders not as threats to themselves and others but as beloved children of God who, enlivened by the Spirit, are not only integral members of the community but also a sign and a symptom of a deeper imbalance in the land—an imbalance to which we all contribute and are all responsible for addressing?

All this to say, the wisdom that emerges from regenerative farming isn't simply about farming. It's about learning to see differently. It's about acknowledging that, no matter how large a particular plant becomes, or how expansive its root system, unless we train our senses in new ways, all we will ever be able to see are slightly overgrown shrubs or, worse yet, weeds that need to be eliminated. Just as we stated in the opening chapter on how to do theology, our goal in writing this book was not to tell you everything there is to know about theology or the historical development of doctrine but to provide you with a set of theological lenses that might allow you to develop insight into the world you inhabit. So instead of giving you more information *about* God, our goal was to invite you into a different way of being in the world—to *know* God more deeply.

And this is precisely the gift that constructive theology offers to people of faith in general and students of psychology in particular: a new way of seeing and thus understanding our relationship with the soil beneath our feet, our fellow creatures (human and nonhuman) who inhabit the land along with us, and the God who placed us all in this garden in the first place. Of course, developing new eyes isn't something that happens overnight. It takes time, a great deal of patience, and the relinquishing of our false sense of control. On a more fundamental level, it also involves death. But just as it is with a seed buried deep beneath the ground, dying to our own selves (Gal. 2:20) is the necessary precondition for transformation and growth. Or, to use Paul's words, "What you sow will not come to life unless it dies" (1 Cor. 15:36).

Some may find the topic of death a somewhat depressing note to end on, but it serves as a fitting conclusion to our discussion, for it encapsulates our hopes and prayers for you. Our objective was never to provide you or anyone else with theological cover so that you could pursue business as usual. We hope to initiate the (sometimes painful) process of tilling up the soil of your life so that it might be capable of producing abundant life—for you and for those entrusted to your care. Which raises a question: To what should we compare the person of Christian faith who is studying psychology? That person is like a regenerative farmer who plants a seed in a garden. It grows and becomes a tree, and the wild birds nest in its branches.

May it be so for you.

Acknowledgments

We would both like to thank the students we have had the honor of teaching, the colleagues with whom we are blessed to work, and the mentors who have continued to teach us long after their official roles ended. We would especially like to thank the diverse group of students, mentors, and colleagues who have continually helped us reckon with the kind of privilege we have both inherited as White males. You have remained fiercely committed to dismantling the various systems and structures that often keep us from seeing this privilege. Thank you for your grace, your courage, and most of all your friendship.

We are also grateful to our editor, Bob Hosack, and those at Baker who were enthusiastic about this book from the beginning. We thank them for their guidance and wonderful editorial work that has helped bring this project to completion.

From Kutter. I would like to thank William for his thoughtfulness and patience as a coauthor. Without knowing anything about my writing process, William committed to collaborating with me on this project, and I can only hope that, in retrospect, he is still glad that he did! I could not have picked a better partner in crime. Our interactions over the course of writing this book made me a better theological and psychological thinker; on a much deeper level, they made me a better human. Thanks for all the countless hours you put into this project, even on top of all your other responsibilities and commitments. I would also like to thank Tina Armstrong, who co-teaches the touchstone class at Fuller Seminary with me for all incoming psychology PhD students. Her enthusiasm for this project, along with her willingness to let me make mistakes in the classroom while teaching psychology students, have been critical in shaping my understanding of the role of theology in clinical and research psychology.

Finally, I would like to thank my wife, Jessica, and my three daughters, Callie Kay, Mattie Kate, and Maeve Virginia. It's not easy having a husband and father who writes books and thinks thoughts for a living. I am blessed to have a family that chooses to love me each day knowing full well that a great many of my numerous activities are simply my way of distracting others from truly seeing me.

From William. I would like to extend my deep gratitude to my wife, Kimberly, for her loving support during this writing process. During the process of completing the final chapters and reviewing the drafts of the manuscript, our first child, Liam, was born. Kimi, I continue to be amazed at your strength and resilience. You believed in this book project and offered your encouragement along the way—despite our many sleepless nights with a new baby and my being a full-time student in a doctoral program. I've grown to love you more over these past months as we've embarked on raising our son together, and I've had more joy in this process than I could have imagined. Thank you for grounding me in the things that are important in life.

When Kutter contacted me about the possibility of coauthoring this book, I had a rough outline of a proposal that I had started years ago on a similar topic. But, as things go in the academic world, it was placed on a backburner because of more pressing matters. On comparing our notes, there was almost a complete symmetry between our visions for the book you are now holding in your hands: a constructive theological approach for students studying psychology. I'm immensely grateful to have traveled with him on this journey and thankful for his courage and vision that imagined us collaborating as coauthors. I would not have been able to do it without him, and this project is vastly better than what I could have done on my own. Thank you for the nourishing collaboration and the reminder that theologizing is best done in community.

Index

207

DATE DUE

GAYLORD		PRINTED IN U.S.A.